# ARCHIVAL AND SPECIAL COLLECTIONS FACILITIES

*Guidelines for Archivists, Librarians, Architects, and Engineers*

Edited by Michele F. Pacifico and Thomas P. Wilsted

SOCIETY OF
**American Archivists**
CHICAGO

The Society of American Archivists is grateful to the Spacesaver Corporation for providing funds to support the development and printing of this publication.

**Society of American Archivists**
www.archivists.org

© 2009 by the Society of American Archivists. All rights reserved.

Printed in the U.S.A. by IPC Print Services, St. Joseph, Michigan.

*Archival and Special Collections Facilities: Guidelines for Archivists, Librarians, Architects, and Engineers* was officially adopted as a standard by the Council of the Society of American Archivists (SAA) in February 2009, following review by the SAA Task Force on Archival Facilities Guidelines, the SAA Standards Committee, and the general archives, conservation, library, and building professions.

**Library of Congress Cataloging-in-Publication Data**
Archival and special collections facilities : guidelines for archivists, librarians, architects, and engineers / SAA Standards Committee, SAA Task Force on Archival Facilities Guidelines ; edited by Michele F. Pacifico and Thomas P. Wilsted.
  p. cm.
Includes bibliographical references and index.
ISBN 1-931666-31-8 (alk. paper)
  1. Archive buildings—United States—Design and construction. 2. Archive buildings—Remodeling—United States. 3. Archive buildings—United States—Planning. 4. Archival materials—Conservation and restoration—United States. 5. Archives—United States—Administration. I. Pacifico, Michele F. II. Wilsted, Thomas. III. Society of American Archivists. Task Force on Archival Facilities Guidelines.
  CD981.A695 2009
  027—dc22
                              2009025386

**Cover Photographs (left to right):**
*Row 1:*
Southwest Façade at Night, Georgia Archives, Morrow, Georgia.
Mobile Shelving Installation, Presbyterian Historical Society, Philadelphia, Pennsylvania.
*Row 2:*
Conservation Laboratory, American Philosophical Society, Philadelphia, Pennsylvania (Barry Halkin, Photographer).
Fire Pump Room, Harry Ransom Center, The University of Texas at Austin, Austin, Texas (James Stroud, Photographer).
*Row 3:*
Building construction, City of Portland Archives and Records Center, Portland, Oregon.
Reading Room, Arthur and Elizabeth Schlesinger Library for the Study of Women in America, Racliffe Institute for Advanced Study, Harvard University, Cambridge, Massachusetts.
*Row 4:*
Mobile shelving, Rare Collections Library, State Library of Pennsylvania, Harrisburg, Pennsylvania (photo provided courtesy of Spacesaver Corporation).
Processing and staff area, Delaware Public Archives, Dover, Delaware.
HOK Architecture, building model for Archives II, National Archives and Records Administration, College Park, Maryland.

Designed by Sweeney Design, kasween@sbcglobal.net.

# TABLE OF CONTENTS

Foreword ........................................................... vii

Introduction ......................................................... 1

## Section 1—Building Site

    1.1    Rationale ................................................. 7
    1.2    Site Selection ............................................ 7
    1.3    Site Evaluation ......................................... 10
    1.4    Site Design ............................................. 13

## Section 2—Building Construction

    2.1    Rationale ............................................... 19
    2.2    Location ............................................... 20
    2.3    Environmental Issues: Below Ground and Cave Construction ............................................. 21
    2.4    Building Structure ..................................... 23
    2.5    Roof ................................................... 25
    2.6    Mechanical Systems .................................... 27
    2.7    Electrical Systems ...................................... 29
    2.8    Commissioning ........................................ 30

## Section 3—Archival Environments

    3.1    Rationale ............................................... 31
    3.2    Paper-Based Records ................................... 32
    3.3    Film-Based Records .................................... 34

| 3.4 | Electronic Records | 35 |
| 3.5 | Environmental Mechanical Systems (HVAC) | 37 |
| 3.6 | Fluctuations in Climate Conditions | 38 |
| 3.7 | Air Filtration | 39 |
| 3.8 | HVAC System Electronic Controls | 43 |

## Section 4—Fire Protection

| 4.1 | Rationale | 45 |
| 4.2 | Fire Risk Assessment | 46 |
| 4.3 | Building Construction | 46 |
| 4.4 | Stack Construction | 47 |
| 4.5 | Mechanical Systems | 49 |
| 4.6 | Electrical Systems | 50 |
| 4.7 | Fire Detection and Alarm | 51 |
| 4.8 | Fire Suppression | 52 |
| 4.9 | Low Oxygen System | 55 |

## Section 5—Security

| 5.1 | Rationale | 57 |
| 5.2 | Security Risk Assessment | 58 |
| 5.3 | External Security | 58 |
| 5.4 | Stacks Security | 61 |
| 5.5 | Loading Dock | 64 |
| 5.6 | Reading Room Security | 64 |
| 5.7 | Exhibits | 66 |
| 5.8 | Physical Security Systems | 67 |

## Section 6—Lighting

| 6.1 | Rationale | 75 |
| 6.2 | Stacks | 82 |

| | | | |
|---|---|---|---|
| 6.3 | Mixed-Use Spaces | | 83 |
| 6.4 | Reading Room(s) | | 87 |
| 6.5 | Public Spaces | | 89 |
| 6.6 | Staff Spaces | | 91 |
| 6.7 | Non-Public Spaces | | 92 |
| 6.8 | General Spaces | | 93 |

**Section 7—Materials and Finishes**

| | | | |
|---|---|---|---|
| 7.1 | Rationale | | 95 |
| 7.2 | External Building Materials | | 97 |
| 7.3 | Stacks | | 98 |
| 7.4 | Processing Areas, Exhibit Galleries, Holding Areas, and Other Areas Where Archival Collections Are Temporarily Stored, Processed, or Displayed | | 107 |
| 7.5 | Exhibit Cases | | 112 |
| 7.6 | Laboratory(s) | | 115 |
| 7.7 | Reading Room(s) | | 118 |
| 7.8 | Mitigation Strategies | | 120 |

**Section 8—Storage Equipment**

| | | | |
|---|---|---|---|
| 8.1 | Rationale | | 123 |
| 8.2 | Shelving Systems | | 123 |
| 8.3 | Materials and Finishes | | 124 |
| 8.4 | Construction and Performance | | 124 |
| 8.5 | Layout | | 126 |
| 8.6 | Dimensions | | 128 |
| 8.7 | Accessories | | 130 |
| 8.8 | Oversized Records | | 130 |
| 8.9 | Cold Storage Shelving | | 131 |
| 8.10 | Cabinets | | 131 |

## Section 9—Functional Spaces

| 9.1 | Rationale | 133 |
| 9.2 | Loading Dock | 134 |
| 9.3 | Receiving | 136 |
| 9.4 | Supply Storage | 137 |
| 9.5 | Service Corridors | 138 |
| 9.6 | Elevators | 138 |
| 9.7 | Laboratory(s) | 139 |
| 9.8 | Reformatting Lab | 142 |
| 9.9 | Processing Room(s) | 142 |
| 9.10 | Computer Room | 143 |
| 9.11 | Staff Spaces | 144 |
| 9.12 | Reading Room(s) | 145 |
| 9.13 | Public Spaces | 149 |
| 9.14 | Exhibition | 153 |

## Appendices

| A – Prohibited Materials | 155 |
| B – Glossary | 157 |
| C – Bibliography | 163 |

Index ............................................................. 179

# FOREWORD

*Archival and Special Collections Facilities: Guidelines for Archivists, Librarians, Architects, and Engineers* reflects the ongoing commitment by the Society of American Archivists (SAA) to produce useful and timely works that help archivists to serve as good stewards of their valuable collections. It is an excellent companion piece to Thomas P. Wilsted's *Planning New and Remodeled Archival Facilities* (SAA, 2007), and also builds upon the brief facilities management discussion in Michael Kurtz's Archival Fundamentals Series II manual, *Managing Archival and Manuscript Repositories* (SAA, 2004).

Professionals have long recognized the need for these guidelines for several reasons. All archivists eventually confront issues related to building planning and/or renovation. They often encounter a bewildering and incomplete array of advice and standards scattered throughout a broad range of professional, trade association, and institution-specific sources. This situation can make it difficult for archivists to communicate effectively with architects and builders. Further, unlike the situation in nations ranging from Australia to Finland to France, no generally accepted national standards exist for archival facilities in the United States.

This book begins to remedy that problem. The co-editors appear particularly well-suited to undertake this project. Tom Wilsted, in addition to authoring a book on facilities and managing several building projects throughout his distinguished career, has long been in the forefront of advocating stronger managerial skills for archivists. Michele F. Pacifico, an experienced consultant who played a key role in planning and designing the National Archives' Archives II building in College Park, Maryland, has published widely in the archival literature over the past several decades. They have assembled an impressive team of preservationists, architects, and archivists to draft and review these guidelines, while also soliciting input from the broader archival profession. The resulting specifications address construction issues, but also stipulate best practices for environmental controls, fire suppression equipment, security, lighting, and equipment. Archivists will undoubtedly consult this as their first step in planning a facilities project, and the extraordinarily helpful bibliography provides a deeper engagement with more specialized topics.

As Wilsted observes in the Introduction, this book really "begins the process of establishing standards that can be used in designing archival facilities." It offers immediate assistance to builders and archivists who are involved with construction and renovation, and it also provides the profession with a baseline for reflection and analysis. In the long run, however, *Archival and Special Collections Facilities* aims to serve as the blueprint for a fully formed national standard. The process of developing official standards is long, arduous, complex, and, for most people, fairly arcane. Fortunately, in the interim, archival professionals now have a well-crafted, easily understandable, thoroughly vetted, and carefully considered set of guidelines that can help them to do their jobs better. SAA is very grateful to all of the individuals who dedicated their time and expertise to make this publication a reality. We hope you make good use of it, and look forward to hearing your comments.

*Peter J. Wosh*
Chair, Publications Board, Society of American Archivists
Director, Archives/Public History Program,
History Department, New York University
June 2009

# INTRODUCTION

Archival facilities are a critical element in preserving and making accessible our nation's cultural heritage. Over the past several decades many new facilities have been designed and built that meet the highest standards for preservation and access. However, it is clear that there is a growing need to improve and upgrade existing structures or replace them with ones that meet twenty-first-century standards. Evidence of these needs is highlighted in the recent *Heritage Health Index on the State of America's Collections* compiled by the Institute of Museum and Library Services. This survey of archives, museums, and libraries published in 2005 found that 26% of institutions surveyed had no environmental controls to prevent heat, light, and moisture damage with half reporting damage to collections as a result. In addition, 59% lacked adequate storage space to house their collections. There is a clear need to address these conditions, but this can only be done when appropriate guidelines are available to those planning upgraded and new archival facilities.

The construction of a new or remodeled archival facility provides the opportunity to address functional building issues and collection preservation and conservation. A purpose built facility offers the greatest flexibility but a well-designed renovation can also meet staff, researcher, and collection needs. Building designers should take a broad view of building needs. While collection preservation is critical, increasingly this function requires less than 50% of the building space and each building area requires careful planning and attention. When planning new and remodeled facilities, archivists and building designers should look at other building successes and at best practices throughout the profession as they work through the planning process.

Successful archival facilities are the result of active involvement of building users and occupants. Archivists must seek broad, active participation in the planning process. Archivists should review printed literature, professional standards, and guidelines, and bring pertinent information to the attention of building designers and ensure that these are incorporated into the building plans. In smaller archives, staff participation may be limited by lack of time and expertise. In such circumstances, staff should make a strong effort to become knowledgeable about building issues. Where time is a concern, they may want to suggest the hiring of one or more consultants to assist with building planning and programming.

The pattern of ignoring archival input in building planning until late in the process has been common and must change. As a primary client and building occupant, archivists have much to add to a successful building design. Each profession—architects, engineers, archivists, and operational and maintenance personnel—has a role to play in the building design. The lack of input from a single profession results in a building that is less functional and that fails to meet the needs of both archival collections and building occupants. Failure to have early and complete involvement by archival staff results in either unnecessary change at later stages in the building process or a less than adequate design. Archivists must not only take the time to become knowledgeable about the building process but use their political skills to ensure their involvement in the planning process.

Standards and guidelines for archival facilities are a critical element in creating or renovating buildings that meet the needs of staff and researchers and ensure the preservation of the collections. The archival facility is the common denominator in the preservation of archival and special collections. Without appropriate facilities and building systems, it is impossible to meet the building's first priority—collection preservation. Archival facilities store paper-based materials but they also contain photographs, maps, multimedia materials and electronically formatted materials. Archival facilities contain unique collections that are usually not replicated elsewhere. They require special environments and security to ensure that material is preserved and protected from theft. The appropriate site, structure, building systems, environmental controls, security, lighting, materials and finishes, equipment, and functional spaces in an archival facility protect the archival collections from deterioration, natural disasters, and theft, provide spaces for collection storage and processing, public programs, staff and researcher use, and ensure adequate space for programmatic and collection growth.

Throughout their discussions, guideline authors discussed how to balance the needs of building designers undertaking renovations versus new, purpose built facilities. A major challenge in meeting the needs of an archival facility is an adequate budget. Building designers are constantly facing a balancing act of requirements and designs that must be evaluated against a fixed budget amount. Such choices require prioritization, but building designers must always keep in mind that collection preservation is the highest priority.

In creating these guidelines we hope that both audiences will find them useful and appropriate. In developing each chapter, we have standardized language to clarify meaning. Throughout the guidelines the authors use a series of terms that indicate the level of importance of any particular issue. These terms are:

- Must = Required
- Should = Highly Recommended
- May = Acceptable
- Not Recommended

Building designers can use this prioritization in making design choices and in evaluating options. With the exception of requirements, building planners must balance archival needs and building requirements with funding available. The result should be a building that is fully functional and meets both collections and staffing and public needs.

American building standards are drawn from a variety of sources. Federal, state, and local governments specify standards that buildings are required to meet. Likewise, specialized building professions also develop standards and guidelines that are required for all or for specific types of buildings. These standards are applied and interpreted by building designers in the course of creating or renovating an archival facility.

While no specific national guidelines or standards currently exist for archival facilities, archivists, architects, and contractors can draw from a number of sources that address aspects of archival design and construction. These include standards developed internationally by the International Organization for Standardization (ISO), the National Information Standards Organization (NISO), and facility standards developed by the National Archives and Records Administration (NARA).

Even with these resources, archivists and building designers often have difficulty in finding and interpreting the different facilities standards. This problem is threefold. The first is that there is no single location or set of archival facility standards that can be consulted by professionals. Archivists and designers must gather information from individual institutional standards and a variety of professional building associations to develop what is often an incomplete set of building criteria. A second problem that designers face is that these standards, delineated by different groups, are not always in agreement. There is often a lack of consensus about specific issues such as temperature, relative humidity, and air filtration levels. This not only causes confusion or indecision, but also encourages designers to ignore standards or select those that are the easiest to meet or the most cost-efficient. A third difficulty in developing standards or guidelines is the United States federal system. Although there are national standards for many building issues, they are used and interpreted at the state and local level using local building codes which can alter their impact and use.

Internationally, a number of countries have already established national standards for archival facilities. Great Britain established a national standard for archival facilities as early as 1977, with the most recent update completed in 2001. Other countries, including Australia, China, Finland, and France, also maintain national standards for either archival or records management facilities. One of the tasks of the committee was to review all existing standards and determine those that should be included in these guidelines. The bibliography cites a select list of standards directly related to archival facilities and the protection of archival records.

*Archival and Special Collections Facilities: Guidelines for Archivists, Librarians, Architects, and Engineers* begins the process of establishing standards that can be used in designing archival facilities. This effort began with the approval of the Society of American Archivists' (SAA) Council through a recommendation of SAA's Standards Committee. SAA created the Task Force on Archival Facilities Guidelines to research and write guidelines. This document will serve the archival profession by providing building designers with a central source of information when designing new or remodeled facilities and serve as the foundation for future standards.

Each section of the guidelines was initially created by one individual. A second task force member reviewed the initial draft and provided comments and suggestions. The entire draft was ultimately reviewed by all task force members. Michele Pacifico and Thomas Wilsted edited the drafts and incorporated pertinent comments and suggestions. The SAA Standards Committee circulated the draft to a number of architects, archivists, conservators, and construction specialists for comment and input. The guidelines were also shared with fellow professionals in the

National Association of Government Archivists and Records Administrators (NAGARA) and the Council of State Archivists (CoSA). The SAA Standards Committee and the SAA Council conducted a final review of the document prior to their approval.

The archival facility guidelines cover the following topics:

- Building Site
- Building Construction
- Archival Environments
- Fire Protection
- Security
- Lighting
- Materials and Finishes
- Storage Equipment
- Functional Spaces

The members of the guidelines' task force represent a number of professional bodies and organizations and each has wide experience in planning and designing archival facilities. They are:

- **Patrick Alexander,** National Archives and Records Administration (Retired)
- **Nick Artim,** President, Heritage Protection Group
- **David Carmicheal,** Director, Georgia Archives
- **Ernest A. Conrad,** President, Landmark Facilities Group
- **Michele F. Pacifico,** Guidelines Co-chair and Co-editor, Archival Facilities Consultant
- **Gregor Trinkaus-Randall,** Preservation Specialist, Massachusetts Board of Library Commissioners
- **Scott C. Teixeira,** Associate, Hartman-Cox Architects
- **Diane L. Vogt-O'Connor,** Chief, Library of Congress Conservation Division
- **Thomas P. Wilsted,** Guidelines Co-chair and Co-editor, Archival Facilities Consultant

The Society of American Archivists will continue to review these guidelines over the next five years and assess their application and value to the profession. This will allow input from archivists, architects, engineers, contactors, and others who apply these guidelines to building design and construction. Ultimately, it is the Society's intent to create a fully developed national standard for archival facilities. Such an effort is time-consuming and rigorous and involves the national standards bodies and many other professionals in the process. The SAA Council, the SAA Standards Committee, and the Facilities Guidelines Task Force view these guidelines as a working document that will grow and evolve over time. We encourage SAA members and others to forward comments, suggestions, changes, and additions as they use this document. Comments will be reviewed and changes to the document made as needed. Comments can be sent to: Ongoing Chair of Facilities Guidelines Task Force or the SAA Standards Committee.

The Committee would like to thank Nancy Kunde, Chair of the SAA Standards Committee, and Nancy Beaumont, Executive Director of SAA, for their initial response and enthusiasm for this project and for the SAA Council's and the Standard Committee's approval and support. In addition, we want to especially thank the Spacesaver Corporation for funding to support the work of the committee, including travel and publications costs.

*Thomas P. Wilsted*

Section 1

# BUILDING SITE

*Scott C. Teixeira*

## 1.1 RATIONALE

Many of the dangers that threaten an archival facility can be avoided by careful site selection. In addition to the normal site considerations of location, cost, and availability, an archivist must take into account factors that provide the safest and most desirable site for their facility. Issues that must be addressed include proximity to water, hazardous materials or locations, and air or ground pollution.

If the site chosen for the facility is undeveloped, careful consideration must be given to precisely where and how the building will be placed on the site. A thoughtfully situated building can be of equal if not greater value to the safety of the facility, its contents, staff, and visitors. Often times, plans may entail renovating, adding on to, or converting an existing structure for use as an archival facility. Archivists and designers should take advantage of such opportunities and undertake important improvements to the site as well.

## 1.2 SITE SELECTION

Site selection for an archival facility must include review of the site's location, size, security, and access. In addition, designers must review and consider environmental conditions and potential impacts to wetlands and other natural resources.

## 1.2.1 Location—Avoidance of Hazards

The site for an archival facility should **NOT** be

- liable to subsidence or flooding, whether from a natural source such as an underground river or from a man-made source such as water mains;

- at risk from earthquakes, tsunamis, or landslides;

- at risk from fire, explosions, or impacts from or related to adjacent/nearby sites, or in adjacent parts of the same building (e.g., within the flight path of an airport or near facilities that handle hazardous materials or cargo);

- near a strategic installation or symbolic site that could be a target in an armed conflict;

- near an industrial or agricultural facility, or other installation emitting harmful gases, smoke, dust, etc.;

- in an especially polluted area;

- on or immediately adjacent to contaminated land, including landfill sites;

- beneath or adjacent to a source of electromagnetic radiation (e.g., high-voltage electrical power transmission lines);

- near a place or a building that attracts rodents or insects.

When some requirements for avoiding hazards to archival facilities cannot be met, a risk assessment should be performed and special provisions made in the project design to protect the facility against such hazards. Designers should keep in mind that the design measures necessary to mitigate site hazards can add significant expense to the project (e.g., contaminated soil remediation).

## 1.2.2 Location—Other Selection Criteria

The site for an archival facility should be

- located within a short response time of emergency services;

- capable of allowing swift evacuation of people in the event of an emergency. Site selection must consider ingress to and egress from the site and the road systems should allow for quick evacuation;

- located on a stand-alone or island site with free access to the entire building perimeter. In cases where the archival facility is within a larger building or cannot stand alone on the site, the facility should be completely protected from dangers posed by the neighboring spaces and buildings;

- accessible to potential users and to cultural and educational institutions;

- accessible by main roads and by public transportation;

- sited so that it is near to, or easily accessible from, the parent organization.

## 1.2.3 Size

These guidelines do not specify a minimum amount of acreage for an archival facility. However, the site must be large enough to accommodate

- the building footprint, including future expansion;

- site access and service roads;

- sufficient parking;

- sufficient tour bus or mass transit loading areas;

- space for required storm water management areas;

- turning radii and maneuvering space for large vehicle—provisions for a 53-foot delivery truck is recommended;

- circulation for trash pickup from designated dumpster areas;

- separation between drop off areas, parking, loading, and the building if recommended as part of a comprehensive security plan.

The site or, in the case of a conversion, the building, should be large enough to accommodate current and projected storage requirements for 15 to 20 years from the date of occupation.

In addition to these projections, further space should be reserved on the site for subsequent expansion.

## 1.2.4 Floodplain Requirements

The entire site should be a minimum of 5 feet [1.5 meters] above and 100 feet [30.5 meters] away from any 100-year floodplain area. If the site, or adjacent sites, contains any land area within the recommended proximity to a 100-year floodplain, then the archival facility should be sited a minimum of 5 feet [1.5 meters] above and 100 feet [30.5 meters] from any 100-year floodplain area, or be protected by an appropriate flood wall that conforms to local or regional building codes.

These recommendations also pertain to ancillary structures on the site supporting the operation of the archival facility. These include a cooling/heating plant, parking garage, storage facility, emergency generator support building, or similar structures.

Up to 50% of the surface parking area may be located within these proximity restrictions (including the floodplain itself) if there are no suitable site alternatives and if the impact of construction in a floodplain or wetland is fully evaluated. Access roads to the facility must not be located on a floodplain and must allow for complete access (360 degrees) to the building perimeter.

## 1.3 SITE EVALUATION

Prior to final selection, technical studies should be completed to thoroughly evaluate sites under consideration for an archival facility.

### 1.3.1 Site Evaluation and Comparison

The National Environmental Policy Act (NEPA) guidelines, while not pertaining specifically to archival facilities, provide a methodology to evaluate site alternatives and provide for an assessment strategy when there are competing sites. An environmental assessment provides an evaluation of wetlands and floodplains, traffic, historic impacts, and other factors. The NEPA guidelines or a similar method for the comparing candidate sites should be employed before finalizing the site selection.

## 1.3.2 Survey

A complete site survey must be performed to include

- boundary/property lines (described by course and distance as well as a written legal description);
- location of improvements (i.e., pavement, buildings, and other structures);
- identification of all easements;
- utilities;
- trees;
- topography;
- legal title search.

The land survey should meet the "Minimum Standard Detail Requirements for ALTA/ACSM Land Title Surveys" as adopted by the American Land Title Association, the American Congress on Surveying and Mapping, and the National Society of Professional Surveyors.

In addition, the adequacy of adjacent land must also be considered in the event of any future expansion of the facility.

## 1.3.2 Geotechnical Investigation

A complete geotechnical investigation should be completed for any site selected for an archival facility. It should address

- depth to bedrock and groundwater;
- soil strata;
- percolations rates;
- pavement and drainage recommendations;
- geothermal activity.

## 1.3.3 Security Risk Assessment

An external security risk assessment must be conducted to determine if there are site-related circumstances that might jeopardize the security of the building by their mere presence, including a multilane highway, a railroad line (active or dormant), a stream or lake, an upstream dam, or the close proximity of buildings or other possible threats. Refer to Section 5 for external security guidelines.

## 1.3.4 Archeological Assessment

For projects located on government-owned land or financed in whole or in part with public funds, an archeological assessment will most likely be required. For archival facilities planned on private land with private funds, an archeological assessment, while not necessarily required, is still recommended since the purpose of an archival facility is in concert with the intent of laws that require such assessments—to safeguard, preserve, and manage cultural resources.

In most cases, when a site is not likely to contain significant artifacts, only the first phase of an assessment, documentation, will be necessary. In situations where there is no legal obligation to conduct an archeological assessment, having this documentation in hand along with the formal recommendations of an archeological consultant can help to quell possible concern about a proposed site, especially in instances where the project must obtain approval through a public hearing process.

The advice of an archeological consultant may also be of value in circumstances where different sites are being considered. If there is a choice between sites having a greater or lesser likelihood of containing archeological artifacts, a great deal of time and expense can be avoided by selecting the site with no or fewer artifacts.

Conversely, if the project site is already known to contain archeological artifacts or if the archeological assessment suggests a strong likelihood that it will, then extra time should be allowed in the project schedule for the archeological work. For example, early-release bid documents for foundation or utility work can be contracted for well in advance of the rest of the project so that if and when artifacts are encountered, the time needed to conduct the required archeological work will not delay the overall project deadline.

## 1.4 SITE DESIGN

Site design must consider building zoning and preservation regulations, energy concerns, security, utilities, and landscaping requirements. In addition circulation, access, transportation infrastructure, and parking have a significant impact on the site design of the facility.

### 1.4.1 Zoning and Historic Preservation Considerations

State and local codes must be followed for all zoning requirements, including setbacks, height, coverage, traffic requirements, open space, and floor area ratios. The local jurisdiction for the project should be consulted for requirements, and a process for public review of the project must be developed. Contact must be made with the highway department of the local jurisdiction, the utility companies, local police, local fire department and fire marshal, the telephone company, and other public works agencies that will provide services to the facility.

If the project is located on land owned by or funded in whole or in part by the federal government and the project site contains historic structures, or if the proposed project impacts a historic district, then Section 106 of the Historic Preservation Act must be considered. Similarly, renovations, alterations, expansions, conversions, or any other modifications to an existing facility utilizing federal funds or located on federal land that might have an adverse impact on other adjacent historic properties will also be considered a potential review project under Section 106. During the evaluation of projects at existing facilities, the potential for historic impact must be evaluated and mitigation strategies developed to deal with any adverse consequences.

While Section 106 of the Historic Preservation Act pertains only to projects on federal land or that utilize federal funds, many states and counties have similar laws that pertain to projects located on government-owned land or funded by government entities. The state and/or local historic preservation office should be consulted in order to gain an understanding of the requirements that will pertain to the project.

For privately funded projects on privately owned land, or for other instances where there is no legal requirement to fulfill special historic preservation objectives, consideration should be given to carrying out the planning process as if it were, since historic preservation laws and the mission of an archival facility have a common goal—the preservation of cultural heritage.

## 1.4.2 Leadership in Energy and Environmental Design (LEED)

If the building project is to be certified through the Leadership in Energy and Environmental Design (LEED) Green Building Rating System of the U.S. Green Building Council, the building's design should first adhere to the guidelines for archival facilities before implementing LEED features for credit.

## 1.4.3 Site Security

Once a site is selected, a comprehensive security risk assessment should be completed as early in the design process as possible so that security recommendations can be incorporated at the beginning of the design process. Refer to Section 5 for security guidelines.

## 1.4.4 Landscaping

The landscaping should be designed for water control, integrated pest management and low maintenance. The landscaping design should

- omit vegetation within 18 inches [.5 meters] of the exterior wall to provide for hardscaping around the perimeter of the building and to reduce the potential for the entrance of pests and insects into the building. This vegetation-free zone must be sloped away from the foundation and consist of gravel or decorative aggregate with appropriate drainage;

- include under story plants no higher than 3 feet [1 meter] tall at maturity, and a tree canopy with limbs at least 7 feet [2 meters] above the ground at maturity to allow light from fixtures to fall on the pedestrian route, so trees and shrubs do not obstruct lighting;

- maintain a minimum of 15 feet [4.5 meters] between building and the drip-line of trees at full maturity;

- in instances of existing buildings and sites, ensure that both canopies and root systems are pruned away from the structure so that they do not overhang the roof, touch the face of the building, or affect the foundation;

- in exceptionally dry and/or windy climates that are prone to wild fires, vegetation should be kept further away from the facility to avoid risk of fire.

## 1.4.5 Pools and Fountains

Pools, fountains, and their related equipment should not be included in the design of an archival facility. These features are not necessary for the operation of an archival facility and pose obvious risk and liability concerns. However, in circumstances where pools, fountains, and their related equipment may already exist on a site or cannot be omitted for reasons beyond the archivist's control, then additional protection against water intrusion must provided. Ideally, if present, water features should be located a minimum of 75 feet [23 meters] from the archival facility and at least 10 feet [3 meters] below the lowest level where archival holdings are located (permanently or temporarily).

## 1.4.6 Site Utilities

### 1.4.6.1 *Water Supply*

Every building must have water supplied from a dependable public or private water main system. Verify the adequacy of the existing water supply at the point of connection or provide acceptable alternatives such as water tanks or towers. Hydrants must be located appropriately to provide the required fire fighting coverage. Adequate pressures must be verified early to determine if any upsizing will be needed to serve the new facility. Metering, backflow prevention, and Post Indicator Valve requirements must be confirmed with the local water authority.

### 1.4.6.2 *Sanitary Sewer*

Cleanouts must be provided on all sanitary sewer and storm drainage lines at approximately 5 feet [1.5 meters] away from the building and at all line bends where manholes are not used. Required horizontal and vertical separations should be maintained throughout the site. Minimum pipe cover and slope requirements should be maintained. On lines longer than 150 feet [45.5 meters], manholes must be provided. Sanitary sewerage should be designed to flow by gravity. Use of sewage ejection systems should be avoided unless absolutely necessary. Sites without public sewer service should be avoided for archival facilities.

### 1.4.6.3 *Storm Drainage System*

The storm drainage system conveys storm water collected on site to an acceptable point of discharge. The storm drains must be separated from sanitary sewers within the property limits, even in cities where separate public systems are not yet available. A storm drainage system may consist of an open system of ditches, channels, and culverts or of a piped system with inlets and manholes.

In most cases, building roof drainage must be collected by the plumbing system and discharged into the storm drains. The storm drainage system on the site should be designed for a 25-year storm frequency, unless local criteria are more stringent.

Storm water design must address any local requirements with regards to water quality and quantity regulations.

### 1.4.6.4 *Electric Power*

The primary power from the network to the building must be run underground in concrete-encased pipe from the property line. All conduits for the primary power must have at least 50% spare conduit (empty) capacity to allow the utility company to pull new power feeds in the event a conductor or power feed fails and must be abandoned in place. Consideration should be given for providing a redundant primary feeder.

### 1.4.6.5 *Telecommunication Systems*

The primary telephone line to the building must be run underground in conduit from the property line.

### 1.4.7 Emergency Vehicle Access

Roads, fire lanes, and parking areas should be designed to permit unrestricted access for emergency vehicles. The entire length of roads, fire lanes, and turn-around must be designed for the weight and turning radius of fire trucks and must provide sufficient width and clearance for emergency vehicle access. The public entrance must be readily accessible to emergency vehicles. At a minimum, one of the long sides of every building must be accessible to the fire department equipment. The designer must review access by fire equipment with the local fire department.

### 1.4.8 Parking/Public Access

Parking, bus drop offs, and parking spaces for persons with disabilities should be designed to accommodate sustained peak visitation periods. Parking and vehicular access areas include

- visitor parking;

- tour and school buses—in addition to planning drop off zones for the loading and unloading of buses, consideration should be given for providing bus parking;

- handicap accessibility—parking for visitors with disabilities (including handicap van parking) shall be provided according to the current applicable federal criteria (Americans with Disabilities Act [ADA]-Architectural Barriers Act [ABA] Accessibility Guidelines), or according to the local Authority Having Jurisdiction, whichever is higher. A fraction of a required space shall be considered as a whole space;

- staff parking—including an appropriate number of handicap accessible parking spaces as required by code.

Section 2

# BUILDING CONSTRUCTION

*Patrick Alexander*

2.1 **RATIONALE**

When constructing an archival facility or when retrofitting an existing building for archival storage, designers must balance the need to protect the archival collections with the requirements of the life safety codes. The life safety codes are designed primarily to ensure that people are protected in the event of fires or emergencies. However, they do not ensure that the building or contents will not be destroyed. Archival construction must protect people but also must provide for a higher level of protection for the archival collections.

Archival facilities must be constructed with noncombustible materials and incorporate fire protection systems and structural systems that avoid catastrophic failure due to an uncontrolled fire, natural disaster, or industrial disaster. The collections in these facilities are permanent and all major systems must be designed with long operating life expectancies. In addition, water leaks are a constant threat to archival holdings so the building construction must implement as many methods as possible to guard against water intrusions. All archival facilities must be fully accessible and comply with the Americans with Disabilities Act (ADA) and any other laws that apply to accessibility.

These guidelines primarily address new construction of archival repositories. It is recognized that many archival collections are housed in buildings that were not and will not be designed as archival repositories and that this practice will continue into the future. For "non-archival" built facilities, retrofitting some of the recommended design features will be difficult. However, if designers review, understand, and apply these recommendations, they can eliminate, alleviate, or mitigate many of the problems inherent in retrofitted facilities.

## 2.2 LOCATION

Archives facilities in the United States have traditionally been constructed above or partially above ground level and the records are generally not stored below ground level. However, more American facilities are looking at all options for archival construction.

### 2.2.1 Ground Level and Above Ground Level Construction

The most common form of construction is buildings with a foundation on or below ground level with the structure mostly at or above ground level. In these circumstances, archival stacks, processing areas, exhibits, and laboratories should be located in the portion of the facility that is constructed at or above ground level. In areas where flooding and/or hurricanes are prevalent, consider locating archival stacks above the ground level.

### 2.2.2 Below Ground Construction

Some facilities are constructed with most of the structure below ground level. In such circumstances, additional waterproofing measures must be provided to prevent water intrusion and moisture infiltration through the foundation and the below ground walls into archival storage spaces. Avoid buildings that require pumps to prevent groundwater from rising into the structure.

Since fire professionals are primarily concerned with life safety and extinguishing the fire, fire fighting activities can result in the flooding of lower levels in the building. Appropriately sized pumping systems that remove water must be provided for archival storage areas and are recommended for all other archival support functions. The pumps must be on an emergency power system so that if normal power is lost the pumps will continue to operate.

Archival stacks, processing areas, exhibits, and laboratories should never be located under parking lots, plazas, driveways, and roadways where traffic can impact the integrity of the roofing system and cause leakage into these rooms. In addition, these archival areas should never be located under gardens or courtyards.

### 2.2.3 Cave Storage

There is a growing interest in the use of caves for the storage for records and artifacts. Cave storage can be created horizontally into the side of a hill or mountain, or with vertical shafts that incorporate horizontal runs for working spaces. Below ground cave storage poses many problems and it is not recommended for archival storage. There are, however, cost benefits that make cave storage an attractive option for administrative and budget personnel.

If used for archival storage, extreme care must be taken to ensure that the caves are not flood prone, or located in areas where there are seismic faults. Potential cave flooding can result from ground water seepage, water used for fire suppression, or from leaks in plumbing and waste water removal systems. Additional measures must be undertaken to prevent water and moisture infiltration into storage areas in cave storage. In addition, fire fighting in a cave can lead to extensive flooding and appropriately sized pumping systems that remove water must be provided for the cave storage. The pumps must be on an emergency power system so that if normal power is lost the pumps will continue to operate.

## 2.3 ENVIRONMENTAL ISSUES: Below Ground and Cave Construction

### 2.3.1 Moisture Control

All exposed surfaces should be sealed to prevent moisture migration. All exposed concrete should be sealed with a low volatile organic compound acrylic membrane curing compound. Floors should be topped with an epoxy coating and walls should be painted. Refer to Section 7.3 for details on the finishes.

### 2.3.2 Dust Control

To properly control dust in cave environments, all interior surfaces should be sealed. Refer to Section 7.3 for details on sealants and finishes. Modifications to the air filtration systems as well as more frequent filter change schedules might be required to keep dust levels low. In both below ground and cave storage environments, positive pressured entrances should be used to keep dust from entering the facility.

### 2.3.3 Mold Control

Appropriate temperature and humidity levels are essential in all archival facilities. Although below ground and cave facilities are less affected by weather, and have more constant temperature and humidity levels, there should be systems in place for measuring and responding to elevated temperature and humidity levels. Mechanical systems that dehumidify must be provided in cave storage environments. Mold growth can be a significant problem in these environments and must be carefully considered when selecting mechanical systems. In addition, since mold growth poses a significant problem to collections and to staff health, plans should be in place to respond to mechanical system failure in a more timely fashion than in normal building environments.

### 2.3.4 Radon Gas

Radon gas can be a significant factor in below ground or cave storage. Testing for the presence of radon gas must be done, and proper mitigating factors such as dilution ventilation must be installed to ensure that the gas does not accumulate in these facilities.

### 2.3.5 Cave Storage Fire Response

When evaluating caves for archival storage, consideration must be given to emergency responses in the event of a variety of incidents. Cave storage sites are typically located in rural areas. Rural sites often depend on volunteers rather than paid emergency response teams that are available on a 24/7 schedule. This could result in slower emergency responses, increasing the potential for higher losses of archival material. It is recommended that automated remote notification systems on all smoke detection and sprinkler systems be used in all archival facilities; however they should be required in facilities in caves and remote areas.

## 2.4 BUILDING STRUCTURE

Archival collections are considered permanent and irreplaceable, and the building structure and systems must be designed with long life expectancies. Structural systems must be of such quality and workmanship that, except for routine repairs and maintenance, the facility will have a useful life of more than 100 years. In particular, the building foundations, exterior and load bearing walls, floors, columns, windows, and roof decking should all be designed with a high level of durability and longevity. Use building materials that reduce the use of volatile organic compounds (VOCs), especially those materials used in construction of the stacks. See Appendix A for a list of prohibited materials. Refer to Section 7 for guidelines on materials and finishes.

### 2.4.1 Building Framing

The recommended building framing materials are steel, masonry, and concrete.

### 2.4.2 Building Envelope

Exterior walls must be of fire resistant durable products like masonry. The building envelope should never be composed of composite wall systems or spray-on or trowel applications over steel and gypsum.

### 2.4.3 Building Interior

Interior systems should be easy to maintain and constructed of durable, fire-resistant products.

### 2.4.4 Building Insulation

Maintaining appropriate environmental conditions for archival storage is dependent on minimizing outside air infiltration. The building envelope should be designed and constructed to minimize or eliminate air infiltration through the walls, windows, doors, and roof to avoid condensation that leads to mold and other environmental problems. Vapor barriers must be installed to prevent condensation in the interior, as well as to prevent condensation on the steel framing. In addition to archival concerns, exterior wall and roof insulation helps conserve energy. Compliance with American Society of Heating, Refrigerating and Air-Conditioning Engineers (ASHRAE) 90.1 is required. Refer to Section 7.3.3 for guidelines on insulation materials.

## 2.4.5 Floor Construction

Floors should be constructed of steel reinforced concrete, and sized to withstand the heavy loads placed upon them by the archival material and its shelving. Typically, open stack floor loads are 150 pounds per square foot [732 kilograms per square meter] or higher while mobile shelving system floor loads are 250 pounds per square foot [1,221 kilograms per square meter] or higher. High bay storage will increase the floor load requirements. Super flat concrete floors may be required for some shelving systems.

Structural engineers must determine the proper floor loading based on the storage and shelving requirements. Samples of the storage materials must be weighed to establish the proper floor load requirements. The floor load should be able to hold the collections if they get wet by sprinkler failure or through some unforeseen disaster.

## 2.4.6 Seismic Considerations

Archival buildings must be designed to comply with local seismic codes, and consideration should be given to exceeding the codes whenever possible. Even in areas with low seismic activity, certain features of seismic resistant design add safety from other threats to the building.

## 2.4.7 Fire Protection

Archival facilities must be constructed with noncombustible materials. Exterior and interior elements should be as fire resistant as possible. Refer to Section 4 for fire protection guidelines.

## 2.4.8 Pools and Fountains

Pools and fountains within archival buildings should be avoided. When pools, fountains, or other water features are adjacent or near archival buildings, additional protection against water intrusion should be considered for the facility.

## 2.4.9 Exterior Openings

Precautions should be taken at all exterior openings into the building to prevent animals such as birds, bats, vermin, and insects from entering the building. Special attention should be given to exterior foundation gaps, exterior roll doors, loading dock areas, attic windows, aerators, and floor drains. Refer to Sections 2.6.8 and 9.3.

## 2.5 ROOF

The roofs of archival facilities must be constructed of durable, long-lasting, and noncombustible materials. The roofing membrane and flashing should be designed to be easily accessible for replacement during the life of the building.

### 2.5.1 Roof Slope

Roofing systems that provide little or no slope should be avoided in archival buildings. Roofing systems should be sloped so that water drains away from archival storage areas and designed so that any water ponding is avoided.

### 2.5.2 Roof Drains

Roof drains should not be run over or through any archival spaces. If roof drains pass through archival spaces, supplemental measures must be provided to prevent water leaks including locating the drain pipes in protected and enclosed chases. Roof drains provided to remove rain water and snow melt should be designed and sized for the uncommon weather events. Planners should design drains to 125% of the international plumbing code criteria and should use—at a minimum—a 100-year event parameter.

### 2.5.3 Water Leak Prevention

Water leaks through the roof are a threat to archival collections. The exact location of water leaks is often very difficult to determine in modern roofing systems. Small holes or tears in a roof allows water to penetrate the roof membrane in one location, and then travel a considerable distance until it locates a crack in the concrete structure. As a result, water has been known to travel distances in excess of 50 feet [15 meters] until it finds a means to enter the building. There are several preventative issues to consider when designing a roof system for archival facilities. Refer to Section 2.2.2 for information regarding below ground facilities.

#### 2.5.3.1 *Equipment Placement*

Equipment should not be placed on the roof. Equipment on roofs can damage the roofing system. In addition, the necessary maintenance activity, including the walking to and from roof equipment locations, stresses the roofing system. If equipment must be placed on the roof, it should not be located over stacks, processing, exhibition, or laboratory areas.

#### 2.5.3.2 *Roof Penetrations*

Roof penetrations should not be made over stacks, and when possible should not be made over processing, exhibit, or laboratory areas.

#### 2.5.3.3 *Skylights*

Skylights and sloped windows should not be located over stacks, or processing, exhibit, and laboratory areas.

#### 2.5.3.4 *Water Sensors*

Install water sensors in the stacks to detect leaks in the roof and sprinkler systems. If necessary, install water sensors in mechanical spaces and bathrooms located over stacks. These alarms should be directly connected to a central monitoring station. Refer to Section 2.6.2 for guidelines on location of mechanical systems.

## 2.6 MECHANICAL SYSTEMS

Proper building maintenance is a key component in maximizing the useful life of a building and properly maintaining archival conditions. Access for service and replacement must be provided for all of the building's systems, including mechanical, plumbing, electrical, fire protection, and security. A building should be designed so that its components are accessible without entering archival storage spaces except for those specifically located within the archival space (lighting, fire and smoke alarm components, sprinkler piping and heads, etc.).

The mechanical systems in an archival facility provide a safe, clean, and healthy environment for the building's occupants and ensure the preservation of its collections. The systems should be durable, designed for energy efficiency, and allow for ease of maintenance.

### 2.6.1 Design Criteria

The mechanical systems for an archival facility should be designed so that the environmental criteria are achieved and not compromised at any time.

- In larger facilities, stacks and other critical areas should be served from a separate, dedicated Heating, Ventilation, and Air-Conditioning (HVAC) system(s) than those serving the rest of the facility.

- Stacks, processing areas, and exhibits must be isolated from sources of pollutants, such as the loading dock, machine rooms, or spaces where cooking, painting, exhibit production, and other such activities take place.

- The entire building should be under positive air pressure. In particular, stacks should be kept under positive air pressure.

- Areas such as the loading dock, food preparation areas, and exhibit production areas should be kept under negative pressure in relation to adjacent spaces.

- The building envelope should be airtight with fresh air, outside air, and make-up air controlled through the mechanical system.

### 2.6.2 Location

Mechanical spaces and water piping should not be located above or adjacent to stacks. Leaks in mechanical spaces are common, and even with optimum waterproofing, liquids can enter adjacent areas. If a mechanical room must be located above a stack, then additional water proofing measures must be installed, up to and including a "roofing" system with appropriate drains under the mechanical room that removes any water that leaks through the mechanical room floor. Install water sensors in the stacks to detect leaks that might originate from the roof, mechanical spaces, or bathrooms. If appropriate, consider installing water sensors in mechanical spaces for early leak detection.

When mechanical rooms are located adjacent to stacks, special precautions should be taken to guard against water infiltration through walls. Walls should be water proofed and additional floor drains installed to rapidly remove any accumulation of water within the mechanical spaces. In addition, depending on the type of mechanical room, vapor barriers in the walls may also be necessary to maintain appropriate environmental conditions in adjacent archival storage areas.

### 2.6.3 Access and Maintenance

Sufficient space should be allocated to allow easy access for expeditious replacement of major components.

### 2.6.4 Exterior Air Intakes

Exterior air intakes should be located to ensure that pollutants do not enter the building air supply. They should be at least 10 feet [3 meters] above grade level. In addition to gaseous pollutants from vehicles and industries, designers should be aware that significant pollution from fertilizers, insecticides, and dust can occur from farm or landscaping activities.

### 2.6.5 Piping

With the exception of fire protection sprinklers, no water, condensate supply or return lines, plumbing, or other water pipes should be run through archival spaces, especially stacks.

### 2.6.6 Equipment Redundancy

HVAC system redundancy in stacks should be considered for archival facilities. This can be accomplished through cross-feeding from chillers, installing additional ducts, or allowing air to be circulated from multiple air handlers. In all cases, spare parts should be stocked to permit more rapid repairs in the event of equipment failure.

### 2.6.7 Loading Dock and Garage Mechanical Systems

A major source of airborne pollutants comes from trucks and vehicle engines idling in garages and loading docks. Whenever these areas are placed within the building, they should be under negative air pressure to prevent combustion gases from entering the building. Refer to Section 9.2 for additional requirements for loading docks.

### 2.6.8 Floor Drains

Screening should be added to all floor drains to prevent insects and vermin from entering the building.

## 2.7 ELECTRICAL SYSTEMS

The design of the electrical system should take into account the overall energy consumption of the building. Consideration should be given to providing spare conduits, breakers, and power distribution capacity in all systems (standard and emergency power) to provide for future changes. Provide empty conduits and junctions with pull strings for future connections. In addition, consideration should be given to providing for 150% of calculated power needs.

### 2.7.1 Emergency Power Generator

A standby generator for emergency power should be supplied for archival facilities. Emergency power should be provided for the following functions:

- Egress and exit lighting
- Fire alarm system

- Smoke control system
- Fire pump

## 2.8 COMMISSIONING

Building commissioning provides documented confirmation that the building systems function according to design criteria and perform interactively according to the design intent and the owner's operational needs. Consider using an independent commissioning agent to monitor the installation of the systems and to oversee the start up testing and balancing of the systems.

Section 3

# ARCHIVAL ENVIRONMENTS

*Ernest A. Conrad*

3.1 **RATIONALE**

The most important preservation measure for archival materials is to provide the best possible storage conditions. All archival records are subject to deterioration over time due to such factors as heat, humidity, harmful particulates and fumes, and frequency of handling. The materials in archival collections are fragile and are subject to chemical, biological, and physical damage. Proper environmental conditions are necessary for the long-term care and protection of the collections. It is crucial to take measures to maintain stable and constant temperature and relative humidity levels and remove damaging particulate materials and gases from the air.

Environmental control systems function to minimize archival deterioration by controlling temperature, relative humidity, airborne particulates, and gaseous contaminants in stacks and other areas where these records are temporarily stored. The control systems should be designed to provide specific requirements with a high level of durability. Controlling access to stacks and restricting stacks to the storage of records further aids in the preservation of the archival materials. Stacks must only be used for the storage of collections. Staff work areas must be located outside stacks to reduce fluctuations in climate conditions and the introduction of pollutants.

In general, most archival materials holdings can be divided into three categories: paper-based, film-based, and electronic-based materials. However, many archival collections have holdings made of other materials, including leather, metal and metal processed images, glass plates, and wax cylinders. These records may require different environments because of their special properties and they should be evaluated separately and given the appropriate storage conditions. Table 3-1 specifies recommended environmental criteria for archival facilities.

## 3.2 PAPER-BASED RECORDS

### 3.2.1 Long-Term Cold Storage

**Recommended:** 50 degrees Fahrenheit [10 degrees Celsius]/ 30% Relative Humidity

For paper-based records, colder temperatures are better for their long-term preservation and the relative humidity must be coordinated to avoid hitting dew points. Higher temperatures will accelerate the rate of deterioration in paper. For example, increases of 9°F [5°C] will double the chemical action in cellulose materials. The optimal long term storage environment recommended for paper-based documents is 50°F [10°C] and 30% RH. This environment is appropriate for documents intended for permanent storage. Records stored at this temperature should only be accessed for copying and conservation work. If a document stored at cold conditions must be used in higher temperatures, it should first be acclimatized by warming it to 60°F [15.5°C] in a sealed container or a climate controlled acclimatizing chamber.

Current research indicates that the best environment for the long term preservation of paper-based records is 50°F [10°C] and 30% RH. These environmental conditions are not easily obtained and are costly to produce as a constant year-round environment. These environments require special Heating, Ventilation, and Air-Conditioning (HVAC) machinery which uses desiccants and computer logic to maintain these low levels year-round. Therefore, long-term cold storage is usually done in smaller stacks measuring less than 5,000 square feet [465.5 square meters].

### 3.2.2 Limited-Access Storage

**Recommended:** 60 degrees Fahrenheit [15.5 degrees Celsius]/ 30% to 50% Relative Humidity

For paper-based documents that need occasional rapid (less than one hour) access for researchers or for other work that requires handling, it is better to store these documents in closed stacks at a slightly higher environment of 60°F [15.5°C] and 30% RH to 50% RH. The lower relative humidity of 30% is preferred.

These environmental conditions avoid the need to gradually acclimatize a document prior to it being introduced from storage to a working environment that can have temperatures up to 75°F [23.9°C] and above 45% RH. Surface condensation would likely occur on a document being stored at 50°F [10°C] when it is introduced to a much warmer room. A document that is stored at 60°F [15.5°C] can safely be introduced into warmer environments as long as the room's environment is no higher than 75°F [23.9°C] and 60% RH. If the room's conditions are above 75°F [23.9°C]/60% RH, then the document should first be acclimatized in a dedicated acclimatization chamber.

### 3.2.3 Mixed-Use Storage

**Recommended:** 65 to 75 degrees Fahrenheit [18.3 to 23.9 degrees Celsius]/30% to 45% Relative Humidity

In processing rooms, reading rooms, and open stacks, occupant comfort and building construction limitations will dictate the room's environmental conditions. However, cooler and dryer conditions should be used as much as is practicable within design parameters. The cooler room temperature of 65°F [18.3°C] is preferable. Humidity levels should never drop below 30% RH or above 60% RH.

For every one degree Fahrenheit of temperature reduction, the relative humidity will increase by 2%. Therefore, in northern climates records should be kept cooler in winter months; maintaining the relative humidity at or above 30% RH will reduce the risk of condensation on the building features.

## 3.2.4 Exhibit Environment—Mixed-Use Spaces

**Recommended:** 68 to 72 degrees Fahrenheit [20 to 22.2 degrees Celsius] /50% Relative Humidity

Exhibition spaces are both temporary display areas for archival materials and gathering places for people. It is important that these spaces be used for collections exhibition on a short-term basis because their environmental conditions will be limited and not provide the best preservation environment for the records. As a compromise, exhibition spaces should have a year-round temperature of 68 to 72°F [20 to 22.2°C] and a year-round relative humidity of 50 RH +/- 5%.

## 3.3 FILM-BASED RECORDS

Film-based records require specific preservation environments depending on their material composition and physical condition. Sensitive films are often stored in specially designed vaults that measure less than 500 square feet [46.5 square meters] and are capable of achieving almost any environmental conditions required for preservation.

The storage of cellulose nitrates is strictly governed by Occupational Safety and Health Administration (OSHA) safety standards because of their highly flammable characteristics. Similarly, cellulose acetates are prone to off gassing hydrocarbons, which can damage other materials around them. Consequently, cellulose acetates are often kept isolated and placed in a cold storage environment with special carbon filtration to minimize the concentration of these harmful hydrocarbons.

The following are the International Organization for Standardization (ISO) recommended criteria for film-based records:

### 3.3.1 Nitrate-Base Film

36°F [2.2°C]     30% RH

### 3.3.2 Acetate-Base Photographic Film

- Black & white
  40°F [4.4°C] maximum/50% RH maximum

- Color
  40°F [4.4°C] maximum/50% RH maximum

### 3.3.3 Polyester-Base Photographic Film

- Black & white
  54°F [12.2°C] maximum/50% RH maximum

- Color
  40°F [4.4°C] maximum/50% RH maximum

### 3.3.4 Photographic Paper Prints

- Black & white
  64°F [17.8°C] maximum/50% RH maximum

- Color
  27°F [-2.8°C] maximum/50% RH maximum
  or
  36°F [2.2°C] maximum/40% RH maximum

### 3.3.4 Inkjet Prints

40°F [4.4°C] maximum/50% RH maximum

### 3.3.5 Glass Plates

60°F [15.5°C] maximum/50% RH maximum

## 3.4 ELECTRONIC RECORDS

Electronic records require specific preservation environments depending on their material composition and physical condition. Recommended conditions are:

### 3.4.1 Acetate Magnetic Tape

50°F [10°C] maximum/50% RH maximum—do not freeze

## Table 3-1 Environmental Criteria for Archival Facilities

| Space Type | Space Name | Temperature | Relative Humidity | MERV Filtration | Dust Filtration | Notes |
|---|---|---|---|---|---|---|
| **Stacks** | | | | | | |
| | Cold Storage | 50°F [10°C] | 30% | 18 | HEPA + Gas | limited access |
| | Paper Records | 60°F [15.5°C] | 30–50% | 17 | HEPA + Gas | active storage |
| | Films | see 3.2 | see 3.2 | 17 | HEPA + Gas | |
| | Electronic Records | see 3.3 | see 3.3 | 17 | HEPA + Gas | no magnetic fields |
| **Mixed Use** | | | | | | |
| | Processing Room(s) | 65–75°F [18.3–23.9°C] | 30–50% | 14 | 90% | |
| | Laboratory—Dry | 65–75°F [18.3–23.9°C] | 30–55% | 14 | 90% | 30 day max |
| | Laboratory—Wet | 65–75°F [18.3–23.9°C] | 30–55% | 14 | 90% | 30 day max |
| | Reformatting | 65–75°F [18.3–23.9°C] | 30–55% | 14 | 90% | scanning & microfilm |
| | Laboratory Supplies Storage | 65–75°F [18.3–23.9°C] | 30–55% | 12 | 60–80% | |
| | Exhibit | 68–72°F [20–22.2°C] | 30–50% | 12 | 60–80% | 90 day limit |

### 3.4.2 Polyester Magnetic Tape

50°F [10°C] maximum/50% RH maximum—do not freeze

### 3.4.3 CD & DVD

50°F [10°C] maximum/50% RH maximum—do not freeze

### 3.4.4 Digital Records (Hard Drives)

Digital records are becoming a significant part of archival storage facilities, and current practice is to store the digital data on hard drives.

| | | | | | | |
|---|---|---|---|---|---|---|
| **Reading Rooms** | | | | | | |
| | Textual | 68–72°F [20–22.2°C] | 30–55% | 14 | 90% | occupied |
| | Microfilm | 65–75°F [18.3–23.9°C] | 30–45% | 14 | 90% | |
| | Audiovisual | 65–75°F [18.3–23.9°C] | 30–45% | 14 | 90% | |
| | Records Holding | 65–75°F [18.3–23.9°C] | 30–45% | 14 | 90% | 30 day limit for records |
| **Other** | | | | | | |
| | Lobby | 65–75°F [18.3–23.9°C] | n/a | 10 | 30–60% | buffer space/ vestibule |
| | Smoking Rooms | | | | | prohibited |
| | Loading Dock | 50°F min [10°C] | n/a | | n/a | negative pressure |
| | Receiving and Isolation | 65–75°F [18.3–23.9°C] | 30–55% | 8 | 30% | negative pressure |
| | Auditorium/ Training/Meeting Rooms | 68–75°F [20–23.9°C] | n/a | 8 | 30% | |
| | Food Service/ Lunchroom | 68–75°F [20–23.9°C] | n/a | 8 | 30% | negative pressure |
| | Computer Room | 68–75°F [20–23.9°C] | n/a | 12 | 60–80% | |
| | Staff Spaces | 68–75° [20–23.9°C] | n/a | 12 | 60–80% | |

## 3.5 ENVIRONMENTAL MECHANICAL SYSTEMS (HVAC)

### 3.5.1 Large Stacks

Climate control for large stacks measuring over 25,000 square feet [2,323 square meters] is generally achieved with HVAC systems that use chilled water for cooling and hot water for heating. In general, these systems can produce environments of about 70°F [21.1°C] and 55% RH in summer and heating climates and about 70°F [21.1°C] and 45% RH in winter. These environmental conditions are generally satisfactory for records in storage for periods under 10 years and when the records are paper-based or the modern more-stable films and polyesters. HVAC systems using glycol solutions for chilled water can achieve the lower temperature and relative humidity conditions of 60°F [15.6°C] and 40% RH, which support the long-term indefinite storage of paper-based records as well as many of the film-based records.

### 3.5.2 Small Stacks

Climate control for stacks measuring less than 25,000 square feet [2,323 square meters] can use HVAC systems that use direct expansion cooling (dx) and either hot water or electricity for heating. These systems are available in the commercial market and are reasonably economical to operate. They can produce environments of about 65°F [18.3°C] and 45% RH in summer and heating climates up to 70°F [21.2°C] and 50% RH in winter. These HVAC systems can also produce colder and drier environments in the winter. These environmental conditions are generally satisfactory for the long-term storage of paper-based records as well as many of the modern more-stable films and polyesters.

The HVAC systems designed to achieve a cold storage environment of 50°F [10°C] and 30%RH require special refrigeration equipment. The most common methods employ the use of desiccants in conjunction with dx refrigeration equipment or special dx refrigeration equipment in pre-engineered commercial food-grade walk-in coolers or vaults. On a small scale, a commercial grade refrigerator can be used to achieve the 50°F [10°C]; however, the stored records need to be kept in sealed containers with preconditioned silica gel in order to maintain a stable 30% RH.

## 3.6 FLUCTUATIONS IN CLIMATE CONDITIONS

Various institutions differ in their findings regarding the damaging effects to records because of fluctuations in temperature and relative humidity. The general conclusion is that large fluctuations in temperature or relative humidity can cause irreversible damage to sensitive records, and that climate conditions must be kept constant. The following list shows the current consensus of the allowable fluctuations in relative humidity, from a set point over a 24 hour period, which minimizes damage to records. Fluctuations in temperature are generally easily controlled to +/- 2°F [+/-1.1°C].

### 3.6.1 Environmental Fluctuation Criteria

Current standards of the National Archives and Records Administration (NARA).

Paper textual records

- 65°F max/[18.3°C]    35–45% RH +/- 5%

- Photographic media, black & white non-acetate
  65°F max/[18.3°C]    35% RH +/- 5%

- Photographic media, black & white acetate
  35°F max/[1.7°C]    35% RH +/- 5%

- Photographic media, color
  35°F max/[1.7°C]    35% RH +/- 5%

- Magnetic/electronic media
  46–65°F/[7.2–18.3°C]   35% RH+/- 5%

## 3.7 AIR FILTRATION

Air filtration measures of particulates and gaseous pollutants must be considered for archival facilities, particularly for stacks and other records holding spaces. Filtration is accomplished by introducing filter media into the HVAC system air handler that serves the stack(s). Filtration technology is complex and continues to change. Designers must consider the archival facility's location, size, budget, and design when planning an air filtration system for the preservation of archival materials.

Filtration to remove gaseous pollutants from stacks is especially important in dense urban locations. The majority of the gaseous pollutants are emissions from vehicle exhausts, stationary combustion sources, and other pollution-generating sources consisting of unburned hydrocarbons, elemental carbon, ozone, sulfur dioxide, and nitrogen dioxide. Other gaseous pollutants are a result of the off-gassing of building construction materials, furniture, carpeting, and the collections themselves. All gaseous pollutants are very damaging to records and when possible should be filtered.

Special filtration systems are required for collections that off-gas volatile organic compounds (VOC) such as cellulose nitrate, cellulose acetate microfilm, negatives or film, and some types of paper and plastics. Often these kinds of collections are isolated or stored off site. If collections off-gassing VOCs are stored in an archival facility then the air filtration system must be designed to manage the measured quantities of VOCs produced by these records.

Table 3-2 specifies recommended concentrations of pollutants that are not to be exceeded in stacks and other records holding spaces.

### 3.7.1 Stacks

Air filtration measures must be considered for long term storage stacks.

#### 3.7.1.1 *Airborne particulates*

To filter airborne particulates, including ordinary dusts and fibers, the air handler should contain a pre-filter with a Minimum Efficiency Reporting Rating (MERV) of at least 7 (previous filtration system 30% efficient) and a final filter of at least MERV 14 (previous 95% efficient). These pre-filters are usually an inexpensive throwaway filter measuring 2 to 4 inches [5 to 10 centimeters] deep. Depending on the geographical location of the archive facility and the levels of pollutants, the air handler should also contain a gas phase contaminate filter located downstream from the pre-filter followed by a special high efficiency particulate filter (HEPA).

#### 3.7.1.2 *Gaseous pollutants*

To filter gaseous pollutants, the current research shows that a mixed media gas-phase filter bed of activated carbon and potassium permanganate provides the best removal of these pollutants. These gas-phase filters are approximately 24 inches [61 centimeters] deep and require a larger amount of space within the HVAC system. The gas-phase filters are more costly than the pre-filters to replace and it can be difficult to know when they need replacement. Some suppliers offer a service that can test these filters to determine their useful life.

Downstream from the gas-phase filter, there should then be a final particulate filter with an efficiency of at least MERV 18 (previous system 99.97% efficient or HEPA). This filter is used to remove fine particles from the gas-phase filter and very small particles, such as mold spores and bacteria, from the stack air. These filters are approximately 12 inches [30.5 centimeters] deep and like the gas-phase filters, take up a large amount of space and are more costly to replace. Sometimes a less expensive second pre-filter, with an efficiency of MERV 12 or 14 (previous system 70% to 90%), is placed in the air handler to remove intermediate-sized particulates first and thereby extend the life of the more costly final HEPA filter.

### 3.7.2 Mixed Use

Good quality particulate and gas-phase filtration are important elements in the preservation of archival materials and should be used in areas where records are temporarily stored and used by staff. A reasonable particulate filtration level in mixed-use spaces is MERV 12 (previous system 70%). Using particulate filters with higher efficiency such as the HEPA filters is not practical and does not give much value in occupied spaces. The choice of gas-phase filtration should be based on measured data about pollutants in the local geographical area. A basic approach of using an activated carbon media for gas-phase filtration will go a long way to control hydrocarbons, vehicle exhaust, and ozone.

It is good practice to reserve space in the HVAC system air handler design for future filtration measures as the local pollutant conditions may change.

### 3.7.3 Exhibits

In exhibit spaces the best way to control airborne particulates and gaseous pollutants is to keep the exhibited records in an enclosed case or vitrine. Otherwise, the space should be considered to be the same as an open stack space and incorporate good quality particulate filtration with, at a minimum, activated carbon gas-phase filtration.

**Table 3-2 Recommended Maximum Gaseous Contaminant Concentrations**

| Compounds | National Archives – Stacks | National Archives – Processing Areas | National Archives – Public Spaces | ISO 11299:2003(E) | Thomson 1986 | NRC 1986 | NISO TR01-1995 |
|---|---|---|---|---|---|---|---|
| Sulfur Dioxide ($SO_2$) | 2.7 µg/m³ 1 ppb | 13 µg/m³ 5 ppb | n/a | 5–10 ppb | 10 µg/m³ | 1 µg/m³ 0.4 ppb | 5–10 ppb |
| Oxides of Nitrogen (NOx) | 5 µg/m³ | 25 µg/m³ | n/a | 5–10 ppb | 10 µg/m³ | Best available technology | 5–10 ppb |
| Ozone ($O_3$) | 4 µg/m³ 2 ppb | 13 ppb | n/a | 5–10 ppb | 2 µg/m³ | 2 µg/m³ 1 ppb | 5–10 ppb |
| Formaldehyde | 25 µg/m³ 25 ppb | 61 µg/m³ 49 ppb | 4 ppb max | | | | |
| Acetic Acid | 50 µg/m³ 10 ppb | n/a | 4 ppb max | | | | |

Table 3-2 specifies the recommended concentrations of pollutants that are not to be exceeded in stacks and other records holding spaces by the National Archives and Records Administration (NARA), the International Organization for Standardization (ISO), G. Thomson in The Museum Environment, The Committee on the Preservation of Historical Records of the National Research Council (NRC), and the National Information Standards Organization (NISO). *Note: µg/m³ means micrograms per cubic meter and ppb means parts per billion.*

## 3.8 HVAC SYSTEM ELECTRONIC CONTROLS

HVAC system controls are a key element in achieving a reliable and efficient heating and cooling system in an archival facility. As the brains of the HVAC system's operation, the controls make all the decisions about when to add or remove heat or change the humidity. Especially for humidity control, the only way to produce stable environmental conditions is through the use of computer-based control systems. These systems provide the only equipment that can perform the complex calculations about the relationship between moisture and temperature in a space.

It is important to specify a control system that is matched to the user's complexity of requirements. In general, it is best to purchase a system that is industry generic so that it can be serviced by any knowledgeable technician. The control system should be user friendly with good graphic displays; able to track and measure all system functions for at least one year; and be web based for remote access and diagnostics.

Section 4

# FIRE PROTECTION

*Nick Artim*

4.1 **RATIONALE**

The speed and totality of a fire's destructive forces represent one of the most significant threats to archives. In a relatively short time period a fire's impact can cause serious structural damage to the facility and may damage the collections beyond recovery. Archival facilities, because of their unique holdings, require a higher level of fire safety than is normally required for commercial buildings. Consequently, these guidelines supplement the mandated building and fire codes for commercial buildings.

Fire safety and building technologies are constantly evolving. Therefore, these guidelines are not intended to prevent the use of systems, methods, or devices of equivalent or superior quality, strength, fire resistance, effectiveness, durability, and safety. Where alternatives are proposed it must be the responsibility of the design professional or equipment supplier to submit technically appropriate documentation to demonstrate equivalency.

Fire safety objectives must be set for the facility. They must establish acceptable loss levels and subsequent protection levels for collections, the building, and continuity of operations.

- Life safety must not be less than prescribed by mandated local, state, provincial, or federal codes and standards.

- The fire detection and alarm system must include Americans with Disabilities Act (ADA) features and functionality.

- Archives must be provided with a reasonable level of protection against damage or loss from fire, combustion products and fire suppression actions. This protection level may vary depending on the unique aspects of specific collections, items, and categories.

- The facility must be provided with protection against catastrophic loss of integrity from fire, combustion products, and fire suppression actions.

- The archives program must be reasonably protected against operational downtime and impact from fire, combustion products, and fire suppression actions. The acceptable period of downtime must be defined by the archives administrator.

- The archives facility must be designated a smoke-free building.

## 4.2 FIRE RISK ASSESSMENT

A fire risk assessment must be conducted when planning a new facility or major renovation to an existing facility. This assessment must identify potential fire threats and their potential impact on the facility, collections, organizational mission, and persons within the structure. It must also evaluate fire protection elements, identifying appropriate solutions that achieve the desired fire safety goals and objectives. It is recommended that a risk assessment be conducted for existing facilities every five years to maintain a continued level of fire safety. This risk assessment should be undertaken by someone experienced in archives fire safety such as a fire protection engineer, insurance representative, fire or building official, or other technically qualified person.

## 4.3 BUILDING CONSTRUCTION

The building provides the enclosure that safeguards the collections and related operations from weather, adverse environmental conditions, and security threats. Protecting the repository from fire damage is paramount. Construction requirements for the repository must comply with National Fire Protection Association (NFPA) #232, *Standard for the Protection of Records and Storage*, NFPA #909, *Code for the Protection of Cultural*

*Resources* and the local mandated building code. Where conflicts between the codes arise the most restrictive requirements must apply for archival facilities.

Critical fire safe aspects of the facility must include

- water supply to the site and building;

- fire detection, fire suppression, and fire alarms systems;

- properly rated construction and roof materials;

- fire rated doors;

- preventing fire ignition from mechanical and electrical systems;

- preventing fire ignition by selecting furniture and finishes that lower flame spread and smoke generation and are constructed with a low flame spread rating;

- isolating fire and smoke to prescribed areas of a floor of the building. Compartmentalizing building spaces will prevent migration of fire and will vary depending on how the spaces are used;

- isolating fire and smoke to the floor where the fire occurs;

- preventing fire spread from an adjacent building or outside sources into the facility.

## 4.4 STACK CONSTRUCTION

Stacks must have the highest level of fire safe integrity. Stacks and areas housing archival materials must be constructed to resist the entry of fire, smoke, water, and toxic gases. Refer to Sections 2.3 and 2.4 for construction guidelines.

### 4.4.1 Structure

All walls, ceilings, and floors of a stack must be constructed of masonry. Combustible materials shall not be used in any portion of the stack's construction, finishes, or any portion of the building's structural members that support the stack. In addition, stacks and all supporting structures must be designed and constructed to ensure that the structure will withstand all the conditions that a fire may impose upon it for the entire fire duration.

The duration of the stack fire resistance must not be less than 1.5 times the anticipated fire duration of all combustibles within the stack. In the absence of accurate knowledge regarding the fire duration, the stack enclosure must not be less than four hours. Stack fire resistance must not be reduced if fire suppression is provided even when permitted by the building code.

All building structural members that support stacks must have a fire resistance rating at least equal to that of the stack enclosure. In a nonfire-resistive building, stacks shall be ground supported. In addition, the stack's support structure must be of adequate strength to carry the full load of the building structure plus the wet weight of the stack structure and contents.

Spray-on fire proofing materials must not be used in stacks.

Safes, file cabinets, or record containers housing archival records that are housed outside of stacks must have a minimum fire resistance of two hours.

## 4.4.2 Walls

Stack walls must be free from penetrations except for openings that are required for essential systems. Conduit penetrations in stacks must be through walls. Floors and roofs shall not be pierced for conduit.

Exterior walls of stacks must have the same fire rating as interior walls and must be free from penetrations. Exception: Exterior openings that are required for proper ventilation and are fitted with automatic fire and smoke dampers that provide a fire resistance rating equivalent to the wall may be used in archival facilities.

Smoke barrier walls with self-closing doors must be provided for all multiple floor shelving systems in stacks to prevent vertical smoke migration.

All stacks greater than 500 square feet [46.5 square meters] in area must be provided with means to extract smoke directly to the exterior. Extract can be mechanical or passive.

### 4.4.3 Doors

All stack door openings must be protected with fire rated doors with a fire rating in hours equal to the classification of the stack walls. Doors must be listed and labeled in accordance with American National Standards Institute (ANSI)/Underwriters Laboratories (UL) 155, *Tests for Fire Resistance of Vault and File Room Doors*. Stack doors must be equipped with automatic closing devices to maintain the door in a normally closed and latched position.

All other fire doors in the repository must be equipped with automatic closing devices and maintained in a normally closed position. Exception: Where closed doors interfere with normal business operations and smoke detection is provided, they may be held open with magnetic devices that release and close the doors upon activation of the smoke detection system operation.

### 4.4.4 Elevators/Stairways

Elevators, stairways, conveyors, and other shafts must not open directly into stacks. Exception: Stairways, elevators, conveyors, and shafts that are located within the stack and are exclusive for use of the respective space.

## 4.5 MECHANICAL SYSTEMS

Climate control for the stacks must be accomplished by fixed systems. Portable heating, air conditioning, or humidity control equipment must not be used in stacks. Exception: Equipment used for temporary stabilization and recovery may be used in emergency situations.

### 4.5.1 Location

Boilers, furnaces, humidification, dehumidification, air conditioning, and other climate conditioning equipment that serve the stack must not be located within the stack enclosure. In addition, all controls for utilities that serve stacks must be located outside of the stack so that access to the controls does not require entry to the stack.

Ducts and pipes that do not serve the stack must not enter or pass through the stack. Any pipe that serves a stack must have its point of penetration through the wall completely filled with cement or other approved grouting.

### 4.5.2 Mechanical Ducts

All mechanical ducts serving the stack must be provided with an automatic, combined fire and smoke damper that is equipped to completely close the duct opening and shut down fans that serve the duct in the event of fire. The individual damper or combination thereof must provide equivalent fire resistance rating to the stack wall.

Duct smoke detectors should be provided in the supply and return ducts of the air handling systems and be designed to shut down the individual air handler unit if smoke is detected in the system.

There should be a main shut-off of the air handling systems. It should be possible to shut down the air handling system manually and override the automatic controls during a fire emergency. This shut-off switch should be located in the fire control panel.

## 4.6 ELECTRICAL SYSTEMS

All stack wiring must be in conduit and installed in accordance with National Electrical Code (NEC), NFPA #70. All circuits that serve stacks must be fitted with arc-fault circuit interrupters (AFCI). Wiring within stacks must be limited to those necessary for illumination. Electrical and communications cabling that does not serve the respective stack must not pass through the stack. Exception: Power limited circuits as defined by NEC, NFPA #70 for security, fire detection and alarm, and temperature/humidity monitoring. Where a conduit or cable serves the stack, the point of penetration through the wall shall be completely filled with cement or other approved grouting.

The electrical distribution equipment, including communications panels, must not be located within stacks. Stack electrical and lighting circuits must be arranged so that they are de-energized when the stack's main lock is engaged. Automatic timers may be used to shut lights off after thirty minutes.

Exception: Power limited circuits as defined by NEC, NFPA #70 for security, fire detection and alarm, and temperature/humidity monitoring may be used in stacks.

Lighting and electrical power within stacks must only be accomplished by fixed systems. Portable lighting and extension cords must not be used in stacks. Exception: Portable equipment used for temporary stabilization and recovery may be used in emergencies.

## 4.7  FIRE DETECTION AND ALARM

Once a fire starts it must be detected and an alarm sounded. For stacks and other spaces that house archives this detection must be during the fire's incipient (smoldering) phase, prior to the appearance of the visible flames. All archival facilities must have automatic fire detection and alarm systems. The smoke detection/fire alarm system shall be connected to an approved central station monitoring service.

The fire detection and alarm system must be installed and maintained in compliance with the current pamphlet of NFPA #72, *National Fire Alarm Code* and the fire alarm equipment manufacturer's technical requirements.

### 4.7.1  Smoke Detection

The entire repository must be provided with automatic smoke detection. Those portions of the building where smoke detection is not technically feasible, (i.e., areas subject to freezing) should be provided with rate-of-rise thermal detection or other suitable thermal detection.

Smoke detection for stacks must be highly sensitive, capable of detecting smoke obscuration rates of 0.04% or less. Detector spacing in stacks must not exceed 450 square feet [42 square meters] per detector or detection point. A fire protection analysis must be conducted to determine the other areas in the facility where high sensitivity smoke detection is necessary, and the appropriate equipment then provided.

Smoke and other automatic detection devices must be placed to avoid physical impact due to collections access and normal operations.

### 4.7.2 Fire Alarms

All smoke and fire detection devices in stacks must provide annunciation at the fire alarm control panel and all supplemental enunciator panels to indicate the specific stack where smoke or a fire has been detected.

Manual fire alarm call boxes shall be provided throughout the facility, including at all stack egress doors.

## 4.8 FIRE SUPPRESSION

Once the fire has been detected it must be extinguished to limit damage to archival collections and the facility. If the fire is detected while it is small and a trained person is present, it may be controlled with a portable fire extinguisher or other similar manual fire fighting tool. However once the fire exceeds approximately 3 feet [1 meter] in height, professional fire fighters are required to extinguish the fire. Automatic fire suppression systems can identify a developing fire and respond within minutes to isolate the fire's size until the fire department arrives.

### 4.8.1 Manual Fire Fighting Systems

All floor areas must be provided with portable fire extinguishers that are appropriate for the anticipated fire scenario. Fire extinguishers shall be installed in accordance with the current pamphlet of NFPA #10, *Standard for Portable Fire Extinguishers.*

A minimum of one portable fire extinguisher for Class A (ordinary combustibles) fires shall be located within each stack and within 25 feet [8.2 meters] of the stack door. For multiple tiered stacks a minimum of one fire extinguisher must be located on each tier.

Fire department standpipe systems and fire hoses must be placed outside of the stack to permit the fire department to connect their equipment prior to entering the stack enclosure. This also protects the collections from accidental operation of standpipes and hoses during non-fire conditions.

### 4.8.2 Automatic Fire Fighting Systems

Where required, all fire suppression systems must be designed and installed in accordance with applicable NFPA standards.

- Sprinkler systems: the standard is NFPA #13, *Standard for the Installation of Sprinkler Systems*.

- Water mist systems: the standard is NFPA #750, *Standard for Water Mist Fire Protection Systems*.

- Gas agent systems: the standard is NFPA #2001, *Standard on Clean Agent Fire Extinguishing Systems*.

All fire suppression systems must also comply with NFPA #909, *Standard for Fire Protection of Cultural Properties*. Where performance alternatives to standard fire suppression component placement is necessary to comply with specific facility and/or archives requirements, they must be reviewed and approved by a licensed fire protection engineer.

Automatic fire suppression systems must be technically appropriate for the anticipated fire scenarios. The system must confine substantial thermal damage to an area that does not exceed approximately one-half of the floors where it starts and to a maximum of 1,500 square feet [140 square meters]. Administrators may require smaller damage areas for specific collections.

Sprinkler and water mist fire suppression systems in archival facilities must be wet-pipe or pre-action type systems.

Dry-pipe systems must only be used for spaces that are subject to freezing.

All fire suppression systems must be kept in proper working order in accordance with the applicable standards.

#### 4.8.2.1 *Stacks*

An automatic fire suppression system must be provided for stacks greater than 500 square feet [46.5 square meters] in area. <u>Exception</u>: A space that contains only noncombustible collections including packing or crating materials, noncombustible shelves and cabinets, or where collections are stored in noncombustible cabinets may use a different fire suppression system.

Sprinkler and water mist fire suppression systems in repositories including stacks must be wet-pipe or pre-action type systems. Dry-pipe systems must only be used for spaces that are subject to freezing.

Sprinkler and water mist systems must be individually zoned for each stack and must have dedicated shut-off valves for each stack. All valves must have clear signage indicating the portion of the facility that they control. All security and facilities staff members must be familiar with the location of valves. Each sprinkler zone must be specifically monitored by the fire alarm system, which indicates the zone with an activated sprinkler.

### 4.8.2.2 *Compact Mobile Shelving Systems*

An automatic fire suppression system must be provided for all stacks where compact mobile shelving is used for the storage of collections. Exception: Compact storage that contains only noncombustible collections or collections stored in noncombustible cabinets on the compact system may use a different fire suppression system.

Compact mobile shelving systems that are installed within existing buildings must have the sprinkler system evaluated by a fire protection engineer or other technically qualified person to ensure that the sprinklers are able to provide the proper level of protection. Sprinkler system modifications or appropriate supplemental suppression must be implemented as necessary before installation of the compact shelving.

Compact mobile shelving systems that are installed in new or renovated stacks should consider electrically operated shelving that can automatically go into "fire mode." Upon activation of a smoke detector, water flow alarm, or manual alarm, fire mode allows the shelving rows to automatically separate to create minimum 5-inch aisles. Electric mobile systems can also be programmed to go into fire mode when the archival facility is closed for business.

Fire protection for archival materials stored on compact mobile shelving measuring 8 shelves high (111 inches [2.8 meters] tall) must use a wet-pipe automatic sprinkler system with 165°F [74°C] quick response sprinklers (Response to Intervention [RTI]=50) spaced on a maximum of 100 square feet [9.2 square meters] per sprinkler and with design for a minimum flow density of 0.30 gallons per minute/square foot over the most remote 1500 square feet [140 square meters] of floor area. Designers should consider using lower temperature (135°F [57°C] or 155°F [68°C]) sprinkler heads.

Recent fire tests have shown that high bay electric mobile shelving systems can safely go 30 feet [9 meters] high providing 30 shelves per bay of shelving without the addition of in-rack sprinkler installations as long as Early Suppression Fast Response (ESFR) sprinklers are used and the archival material is stored in boxes. Additional provisions for fire protection on the high bay mobile shelving include 6 inch [15 centimeters] longitudinal flue spaces between the back to back shelving rows and 3 inches [8 centimeters] transverse flue spaces between adjacent shelving units.

4.8.2.3 *Exhibition/Laboratories/Processing/Hold Areas*

An automatic fire suppression system must be provided for all areas where archival materials are exhibited, treated, or temporarily stored.

4.8.2.4 *Cold Storage*

Clean agent systems (gas agent extinguishing system) that comply with NFPA 2001, *Standard on Clean Agent Fire Extinguishing Systems*, or pre-action sprinkler systems must be used in cold stacks and other areas subject to temperatures below 40°F [4.4°C]. When using a clean agent system, the gas manufacturer or authorized distributor must provide proof that the agent has been tested and demonstrate successful fire extinguishment in scenarios that are similar to those in the proposed protected area.

## 4.9 LOW OXYGEN SYSTEM

A Low Oxygen System is a promising emerging technology that currently is used in a few European facilities and is undergoing evaluation by several cultural heritage organizations in North America.

The Low Oxygen System recognizes that fires cannot achieve full flaming combustion when room oxygen levels are below 16% which is less than the nominal 21% oxygen found in air. A smoldering fire may occur that can be detected by a smoke detection system and extinguished with simple methods. However without a source for a flaming fire some of the traditional fire suppression methods, such as sprinklers, may not be needed.

The 16% oxygen level is accomplished by special nitrogen generators that are connected to the building's air handling system. To be successful the room must be relatively air tight. A healthy person can work in this atmosphere for a designated time period without harm.

As the technology advances, this section will provide more specific guidelines.

Section 5

# SECURITY

*Gregor Trinkaus-Randall*

## 5.1 RATIONALE

Security measures must be taken in archival facilities to protect the collections from unauthorized access, change, destruction, or other threats. Maintaining unbroken custody of archival materials is a critical responsibility of every archival institution and unauthorized and unsupervised public access to collections storage must be forbidden. Archives must be rigorously protected against theft, burglary, vandalism, terrorism, unauthorized alteration, other criminal acts, and casual damage or disturbance caused by inexpert or careless handling.

Archival facilities and their budgets vary as do their security needs. It is important, however, that the administrators and staff consider the unique nature of their mission, building, location, and budget when developing a security program. Security programs are often overlooked as a core archival function, and the result can be loss of, or damage to, collections. It is important for archivists to incorporate security steps into their basic archival functions. Some archives may not be able to implement all the suggestions in these guidelines. After careful analysis, choices for security should be based on the feasibility and appropriateness of the security program for the facility and the collections.

Implementing a security program minimizes the possibilities of damage to the facility and damage or loss to the collections. The security program for a new or renovated facility should be developed from the beginning of the building's initial planning and programming efforts. Establish a design that includes layers of security from exterior to interior addressing

- the site and its perimeter;
- the building envelope;
- the building interior;
- the collections.

## 5.2 SECURITY RISK ASSESSMENT

The most effective means of determining the security needs of an archival facility and of each area within the facility is a security risk assessment, also known as a security risk analysis. A security risk assessment examines the outside and inside of the facility and the archival operations. The risk assessment must include stacks, processing, exhibit, loading dock, offices, reading room(s), and public areas security. The assessment results should be incorporated into the site development and facility design (new or renovated). A thorough assessment will result in a design that includes security layering from the outside perimeter of the site to the innermost and most secure stacks.

## 5.3 EXTERNAL SECURITY

The archives facility's overall security needs must be designed to address its site and location. The facility should be located near police and fire services to provide a short response time in case of an emergency. Archival facilities should not be located near a strategic installation or symbolic site that could be a target in an armed conflict. Refer to Section 1.2.1 for guidelines on avoiding hazardous locations.

### 5.3.1 Perimeter

The perimeter and all parts of the facility must be secure against unauthorized entry and vandalism. When location permits, the perimeter of an archival facility should have

- a secure buffer zone around the repository;
- fences;
- security-gates;
- clear illumination in the hours of darkness;
- one visitor entrance.

All means of access to the facility, such as doors, elevators, stairways, windows, and ventilation (duct work/shafts) should be designed to protect against unauthorized entry into the building. Archival material should not be permanently or temporarily stored in areas used as corridors or emergency exits, the loading dock, or the mail room.

### 5.3.2 Building Systems

To minimize unnecessary access by maintenance staff, all building systems must be capable of being isolated and controlled independently. All heating, ventilating, and air-conditioning (HVAC), water and drainage pipes, and electrical controls must be located outside the stacks and must not provide direct access to the stacks. Other services such as gas, oil, and sewage must be located outside the stacks. Security mitigation measures must be taken if these conditions are not achievable for stacks.

Locks must be installed on all master lighting/electrical panels, so that no unauthorized personnel can turn off the lights. If this is not possible, these services should be controlled from outside the facility.

### 5.3.3 Windows

Windows, while aesthetically appealing, present security risks to archival facilities and their collections. In general, archival facilities should have as few windows as practically possible. Additionally, roof lights and skylights should be avoided and must never be installed over stacks or in areas where collections are used or exhibited.

- Stacks: no windows or skylights.
- Exhibit areas: no windows or skylights.

- Processing areas: no windows; if present the windows must be secured and should be double glazed and filtered against excess light and ultraviolet radiation.

- Laboratories: no windows; if present the windows must be secured and should be double glazed and filtered.

- Reading room(s): windows may be permitted, but they must be secured, double-glazed and filtered. In addition, windows should be visible from the reference desk so that they can be monitored.

Windows in an archival facility should be small, not openable, and glazed with strengthened glass. In addition, windows vulnerable to intrusion should be secured with bars, grills, toughened glass, metal roller shutters, intruder sensors, or with a combination of these measures. Windows within 10 feet of grade level should be monitored by sonic glass break detectors or by beam motion detectors. Depending on their location, one-way glass may be used to prevent people from viewing sensitive areas of the facility.

To stabilize the environment, guard against condensation in the repository, and reduce the risks of exposing archival documents to light, all windows into areas where records are exposed should be double-glazed, with an ultraviolet filter incorporated into the glass or provided as a screen or film. In addition, shutters, louvers, blinds, or roof overhangs should be used to shade the windows. In older or retrofitted facilities, stack windows should be blocked to protect collections. Refer to section 6 for lighting guidelines.

## 5.3.4 Exterior Doors

Exterior doors must be strongly constructed, close fitting and equipped with thief-resistant locks. The facility should have an intruder alarm system, which must be connected to a central control unit at the police or security station, and include procedures for servicing alarm calls. In shared premises, internal doors between the archives and other parts of the building must be securely locked when the archival facility is unoccupied. Fire department personnel and security specialists should review the types of locks being used and their system of operation, particularly in the case of electronic or electromagnetic locking devices, to ensure that they meet fire codes and security goals.

Emergency exit doors should be designed to open only from the inside, should open onto an escape route, and comply with fire regulations. Unsupervised emergency exit doors must be equipped with delayed egress locking devices with local alarms. If the local fire code permits, the delay should be set to 30 rather than the standard 15 seconds.

Doors leading out of the closed-access areas must be fitted with locks that may be opened from the inside without a key but can be opened from the outside only with a key or electronic access system. Stacks doors must not be used as external doors of the facility or open into any part of the public-use areas of the facility. Exterior doors left open for public access, deliveries, or staff use must be monitored at all times and should not be located near stack entrances.

## 5.4 STACKS SECURITY

Providing security and controlled access for the stacks begins externally and continues inside the building. Layers of security provide the best protection for the collections in an archival facility. Wall and floor construction must be built to aid the physical security of the stacks. Mechanical, electrical, and fire safety systems must be designed for the physical security of the stacks.

Stacks must be used solely for the storage of collections. Staff work areas must not be located within stacks; the constant passage of staff to and from work areas in stacks compromises their security and their environments. Stack entrances should be located away from public areas of the building. Finally, the doors, locks, and alarms are critical to providing the required security for the collections.

### 5.4.1 Doors

All doors providing access to stacks must be locked and continually monitored. For stacks needing a high level of security, doors require a minimum four-hour fire rating. For other stacks, "custom," rather than "standard," hollow metal doors and frames are recommended because they can be manufactured to any dimension and can accommodate different hardware combinations. Wooden doors and framing should not be used for stacks.

Hollow metal doors and frames are classified in levels:

- Standard (level one)
- Heavy-Duty (level two)
- Extra Heavy-Duty (level three)
- Maximum-Duty (level four).

"Maximum-Duty" doors and frames are recommended for stacks because they are tested to a more rigorous standard, have thicker steel in the door and the frames, are full flush and seamless, have a higher fire rating, and more successfully resist intruders and severe weather. These doors should have at least a two-hour, and preferably a four-hour, fire rating to match the wall rating. All door assemblies should be subject to the following testing as prescribed by the Hollow Metal Manufacturers Association (HMMA):

- Static load testing
- Impact testing (soft body and hard body)
- Vision system impact testing
- Forced entry attack testing
- Jam/wall stiffness testing
- Edge crush testing

Stack doors should only open into areas monitored by and accessed by staff. Stack doors must not exit to the exterior of facility. Exception: Emergency exits may exit to the exterior of the facility.

### 5.4.2 Locks

Locks for stack doors may be manual or electronic depending upon the facility's security requirements, budget, procedures, and other requirements.

Manual locks must have a high security rating and come with interchangeable cores so that they can be re-keyed for new requirements or lost keys. Astragals should be used to shield the locking mechanism. Procedures for managing manual locks are an important component when using them in an archival facility and should include requirements to

- limit the number of keys distributed to staff;

- maintain careful records of key circulation;

- require daily sign-out and return of keys to the stacks, which provides written documentation of who was in the stack areas at specific times and dates;

- ensure the return of all keys when staff leaves archives' employment. Lost or unaccounted keys require replacement and sometimes lock re-keying, which is both expensive and time-consuming.

Electronic locks restrict access to staff using keypad combinations, programmed access control cards, and/or biometric locks. There must be a secure, back-up source of electricity such as an emergency generator, to ensure that the electronic locks do not become unlocked in the event of a power failure. Refer to Section 5.8.2 for details on electronic access control systems.

- With keypad systems there is the risk that too many people may end up with access to the combination. However, it is easy to change combinations as needed.

- Electronic access systems have the advantage of automatically recording the time of staff entry and egress to designated spaces into a central database. Also, lost access cards or a change in staff can be quickly and easily corrected in the system's database.

### 5.4.3 Windows

Windows must not be located in stacks, as they provide a possible entrance and exit point for intruders and allow in damaging natural light.

### 5.4.4 Alarms

In addition to external intrusion alarms, internal intrusion alarms for stacks are important for archival security and include door alarms and a variety of motion detectors. Door alarms should be activated if the door is forced open, not properly closed, or propped open. All alarms must be connected directly to the police or a central monitoring center. In addition, there should be an audible alarm in the facility to alert staff of a possible breach of security. Refer to Section 5.8.4.

## 5.5 LOADING DOCK

It is crucial that security be integrated into the design of the loading dock and receiving room(s).

The loading dock must provide a secure environment for receiving archival materials into the building. Collections must be protected from theft and vandalism, as well as fire, weather and pests.

Loading dock doors, whether roll-up or swing, must have appropriate security. If there is a separate receiving room, it should have the same door security as a stack door.

When materials arrive at the loading dock, they should immediately be screened and moved to appropriate areas. Archival materials should be moved immediately to a secure receiving area. If there is no secure receiving room, the collections should be moved to the stacks soon after they are examined for security risks, pests, and mold. Food should be moved immediately to the food service area; mail moved immediately to the mail room. Screening may be done with a metal detector. Refer to Sections 9.2 and 9.3 for loading dock and receiving functions.

## 5.6 READING ROOM SECURITY

Researchers have direct access to the collections in the reading room where they are at the greatest risk of damage, vandalism, or theft. It is important to address physical security through facility design and carefully established security policies and procedures. Refer to Section 9.12 for the functions and adjacency requirements for reading room(s).

### 5.6.1 Access

Reading room(s) and their support spaces should be accessible from the public entrance and/or lobby of the archival facility. The public should not be permitted to walk through or by stacks and other records holding areas. Researcher registration, also referred to as the sign-in desk, should be located outside the reading room. In a shared facility, it may be necessary to locate the registration operation at the entrance or in the lobby of the facility. Researcher lockers and public restrooms must be located outside the reading room.

There should be one secure entrance/exit to the reading room for researchers and it must be located separately from registration and lockers. There must be no direct access to restrooms or other unsupervised spaces from the reading room.

In a high-profile building or where there are significant concerns about personnel safety and damage to the materials, it may be necessary to install a magnetometer at the reading room entrance or at the entrance to the facility to check for metal objects, such as guns, knives, or razor blades.

Fire and emergency exits should be controlled and provided with alarms, and should never be used for routine access or egress.

### 5.6.2 Layout

The reading room(s) should be designed to provide clear supervision of all researchers by archives staff and/or monitors and contain as few visual barriers as possible. There should be no support columns, stacks, or other large objects such as microfilm readers, desks, or filing cabinets blocking the staff's view of any part of the room. Ideally, there should be a sufficient number of tables to accommodate researchers on only one side of the table with each researcher facing the reading room monitor. If this is not possible, arrange the tables so that the staff can see the researchers' hands and face on both sides of the tables. Assigning multiple researchers to a table (4-top) provides an additional deterrent to theft or damage to the materials when space is a consideration.

Lighting should be adequate to allow staff to monitor the room and allow researchers to carry out their research. The reading room should not have windows that open allowing access from the outside. Windows should be relatively small and located where they are clearly visible from the reference desk. If windows do exist, they need to be sealed and secured through the use of bars or grills; alarms, metal roll shutters, and/or toughened glass with ultraviolet protection. Blinds, shades, or roof overhangs can be used to minimize the amount of light entering the room and provide visual security from the facility's exterior. Natural light should not fall directly on the collections.

### 5.6.3 Access to Collections

Researchers must only be allowed access to collections in the reading room. Only authorized staff must be allowed to access collections in the stacks.

The reading room should be arranged with enough space between tables to permit a cart with archival materials to be placed next to the table. Researchers should be permitted to access a limited amount of material at one time to avoid the possibility of mixing of collections and having the boxes block the staff monitor's view of researcher work.

Collections must not be left in the reading room overnight. When the facility closes for the evening, all collections must be housed in a secure location until the next business day. If space allows, there should be a secure records holding area located adjacent to the reading room to temporarily store records being used by researchers. If no secure hold area is available, the records should be returned to the stacks overnight.

## 5.7 EXHIBITS

Exhibition spaces should be located near other public access areas but must provide security from theft or vandalism for any archival materials on display. Individual exhibit cases must be locked and tamper proof. Cases should be alarmed, which can be accomplished by using a photoelectric beam or an alarm that is set off with contact. For particularly valuable materials or in an open exhibit area, a photoelectric beam should be used.

When the facility is closed, the entire room must be protected by a motion detector.

## 5.8 PHYSICAL SECURITY SYSTEMS

Archives security is dependent on the installation of physical security systems including locks, electronic access control systems, perimeter detection systems, interior detection systems, lighting, alarms, and surveillance equipment. There are a number of variables to consider when determining the best physical security system for a facility, including facility design, location, and budget. Designers and users should consult with a security expert before finalizing security plans.

### 5.8.1 Locks

Since the majority of recorded entries into a facility occur through doors, a quality locking system for both exterior and interior doors is crucial to facility and collection security. No door or lock is impenetrable and together they are no stronger than the weakest point. Table 5-1 specifies recommended locks for archival facilities.

To achieve door security, provide

- a proper-fitting, windowless, hollow metal door located where an intruder cannot use a broken adjoining window to unlock the door from the inside;

- inward-facing hinges. However, if outward-facing hinges are necessary they must have fixed-pins to avoid jimmying;

- high security locks with multiple-pin tumblers, deadlock bolts, interchangeable cores, astragals, and serial numbers.

**Table 5-1 Locks for Archival Facilities**

| Locks | Recommended | Recommended with Reservations | Not Recommended |
|---|---|---|---|
| Double bolt lock | x | | |
| Drop bolt/deadbolt lock | x | | |
| Mortise double cylinder deadbolt lock | x | | |
| Interconnected lock | | x | |
| Mortise or cylinder deadbolt lock | | x | |
| Spring bolt lock | | | x |
| Key-in-the-knob lock | | | x |

### 5.8.2 Electronic Access Control Systems

Electronic access control systems permit entry through a door using a keypad, card, or biometric identifier. Advanced electronic systems go beyond simply locking and unlocking doors and are becoming more commonly used in archival facilities. Any electronic security access control device/system must have a backup power source to guarantee continuity of security in the event of an electrical outage.

#### 5.8.2.1 *Electronic Digital Lock*

An electronic digital lock can use the same door mounting holes as most key locking systems, but the lock is operated by an integrated keypad. A digital lock can be keyless or combined with a key for expanded security. The advantage of a digital lock is that the combination can be easily changed. The disadvantage is that the lock system is limited to a single door, and it cannot record who enters and exits through the door.

#### 5.8.2.2 *Electronic Control System*

An electronic control system uses a card reader at each door requiring controlled access. Available with a variety of features, an electronic control system is centrally controlled and can be programmed to limit access by time of day, by location, and to specific staff. In addition, the system can provide auditing features, remotely administered and controlled access, and expand or limit access without physically re-keying the locks. Lost access cards and terminated staff can quickly be deleted from the system. The audit features allows the computer to maintain access records for each door use and create user histories.

5.8.2.3 *Biometric Identification*

A biometric identification security system measures the physical characteristics of a person to determine authentication and control access. This system can be used on single doors as well as programmed into a card-reading access control system.

5.8.3 **Perimeter Detection Systems**

Perimeter detection systems are designed to detect intrusion through doors, windows, skylights, and other apertures in the facility. They include a number of different devices. Most devices are electromechanical and transmit an alarm if the electrical current moving through the system is interrupted.

5.8.3.1 *Windows*

- Foil tape is often used on panes to protect their windows against vandalism. However, foil tape readily deteriorates, can be easily damaged, and is expensive to install and maintain.

- Glass break detectors attach to windows and contain a small frequency sensor that detects breaking glass. It is quite effective, but the device and wires are visible at all times.

- Audio glass break detectors can be mounted on the wall in a small room with several windows. They are usually connected to the alarm system and are only armed when the alarm system is activated.

- Security screens function like ordinary window screens except that they include tiny interwoven wires that alert the alarm system when the screen is removed or cut. Since they need to be custom made, they are expensive. However, they do permit ventilation, when appropriate, without sacrificing security.

### 5.8.3.2 *Doors*

- A magnetic door contact switch consists of current running through two contacts, one attached to the frame and one attached to the door. When the contact is broken, the alarm sounds. These are very reliable, but they can be bypassed by using a strong magnet.

- A balanced magnetic door contact switch uses a closed magnetic field and unlike the magnetic door contact switch, these units are difficult to bypass. However, they must be precisely mounted, and, since they are matched when manufactured, they are not interchangeable.

- Door prop alarms sound if the door has been left or propped open longer than a set period of time.

- Latch position indicators set off an alarm if the door has not been latched properly.

### 5.8.3.3 *Walls, Windows, and Doors*

Vibration detectors sense movements in walls, windows, doors, skylights, etc. when an intrusion is attempted.

### 5.8.4 Interior Detection Systems

Interior detection systems sound an alarm when an intruder enters a locked facility. Most systems operate by sensing movement in the area. Each system reacts differently and to different situations so designers must determine which system(s) works best for each facility and security program.

### 5.8.4.1 *Mat Switches*

Mat switches consist of two pieces of conductive materials that are kept apart by a material barrier. When weight is placed on the mat, the conductive materials touch, completing an electrical circuit and setting off an alarm. These are often located at archival facility entrance doors.

### 5.8.4.2 *Stress Sensors*

Stress sensors work on the same principle as the mat switches and monitor extra weight being placed in an area. They are often placed on load-bearing beams under areas to be monitored, including roofs.

### 5.8.4.3 *Ultrasonic Devices*

Ultrasonic devices send out a balloon-like pattern of high-energy sound waves that are picked up by a receiver. Interruption of the waves sets off the alarm. These waves cannot penetrate walls so their use is restricted to rooms without interior barriers. They can be used in rooms with multiple doors and windows as long as barriers are not present.

### 5.8.4.4 *Microwave Alarms*

Microwave alarms establish an electromagnetic field that triggers an alarm when disturbed by an intruder. The shape of the field can be adjusted to cover a long corridor or an open space. Microwaves can penetrate wood, glass, drywall, and similar materials so placement is crucial to avoid false alarms. Since they can penetrate walls, etc., they are easier to hide and monitor areas in other rooms. Problems may arise if the beams penetrate exterior walls and respond to exterior movement such as passing vehicular traffic, resulting in false alarms.

### 5.8.4.5 *Photoelectric Beams*

Photoelectric beams transmit infrared or ultraviolet beams to a receiver. They are particularly effective in long corridors or in restricting access to whole sections of a building. They can also be camouflaged as ordinary electrical outlets as well as small boxes on the wall or on a column. Often these are used to protect exhibits, as they can provide a barrier which visitors cannot pass without setting off an alarm.

### 5.8.4.6 *Infrared Sensors*

Passive infrared sensors "examine" an area searching for changes in infrared energy or temperature emitted from objects in the area and set off an alarm when changes occur. These units are sensitive enough to detect changes near an air conditioner or radiator. Therefore, placement is crucial to avoid interference in their field of "vision." These are often used in reading rooms and large stacks.

### 5.8.4.7 Dual Technology Sensors

Dual technology sensors combine the capabilities of ultrasonic devices and passive infrared sensors. Both devices must be activated for an alarm to occur minimizing false alarms. These can often be used in reading rooms and large stacks.

### 5.8.5 Alarms

Security systems rely on two types of alarms: local and silent. Silent alarms are recommended for archival facilities.

- Local alarms set off a loud noise and/or flashing lights when activated. This is designed to cause the intruder to leave the scene and alert the intruder's presence to patrolling police and/or passersby. Such alarms are not effective since they do require immediate police or security response.

- Silent alarms are wired directly to a police department, central monitoring location, alarm company, or campus security. In this instance, the intruder has no knowledge that the alarm has been triggered. Assuming that there is a quick response, there is a better chance of apprehending the intruder.

### 5.8.6 Lighting

Archival facilities should provide enough exterior and interior lighting to prevent dark spaces where intruders could hide. A well-lighted exterior will deter a potential intruder from spending time trying to break into a facility when the risk of being observed is high. Refer to Section 6 for lighting guidelines.

### 5.8.7 Surveillance Equipment

The most common form of surveillance equipment is closed-circuit television (CCTV). CCTV cameras can be installed to monitor the perimeter of the building, exterior doors, the loading dock, stacks, reading room(s), exhibits, public access areas, corridors, and office areas. Camera recording should be motion activated and have system storage adequate to provide a minimum of 30 days of recording. The CCTV system should be supported by a battery backup system or by emergency generator. The system should work in low light conditions of 2.8 foot candles [30 lux]. Refer to Section 6 for lighting guidelines.

CCTV can be effective for observing patrons, but it is not infallible in detecting theft in the reading room. It is difficult for staff to maintain constant TV monitoring, so some archives only use the CCTV when a researcher is suspected of theft or mishandling records.

Section 6

# LIGHTING

## Diane L. Vogt-O'Connor

### 6.1 RATIONALE

Archival facilities must take measures to protect the collections from the damage caused by excessive light levels, ultraviolet (UV) light and infrared (IR) light. Archival lighting must strike a balance between three essential goals:

- *Economical:* Lighting must not greatly increase overall energy usage. Lighting costs should be kept as low as possible and archival facilities should strive toward "green" status.

- *Safety:* Lighting must be filtered and controlled in order to ensure the maximum life expectancy of sensitive archival records and limit their deterioration due to light aging that results in fading, color shift, and darkening of collections.

- *Functional:* Lighting must optimize use of the building features, services, and holdings of archival records and special collections by staff and visitors. Lighting must be planned to support the facilities' environmental, security, safety, and accessibility goals.

Proposals for archival buildings may suggest a variety of lighting sources including daylight, fluorescent lighting, incandescent lighting, and specialty lighting sources such as high intensity xenon arc lighting or light emitting diodes (LED). Not all lighting sources are equally economical, safe, and functional for archival and special collections.

### 6.1.1 Economics

The lighting selected for an archival facility will be impacted by the type of lighting budget that the organization can afford over time. These costs may include

- lighting system purchase and installation—the lighting hardware, lighting lamps (bulbs), filters, diffusers, and software;
- replacement bulb purchase and installation costs;
- ongoing energy costs, as almost a third of a building's power costs are due to lighting;
- the cost of bulb disposal, particularly for mercury and rare metal lamps.

Overall lighting costs may be reduced if care is taken during the design process to analyze the facility's illumination needs and consider the

- ambient lighting set points;
- color balance needs;
- illumination levels and zones filtering needs;
- types of available fixtures and lamps.

Coordinate lighting with room layouts, colors, and surface choices. Lighting design should also take into consideration special needs for color balanced lighting in areas such as conservation laboratories and reformatting areas, special task areas, handicapped accessibility, and needs of older researchers. Energy budgets can be cut substantially by training staff in lighting use and by regularly maintaining lighting systems with the appropriate controls, such as sensors, dimmers, and timers.

Some of the easiest ways to lower lighting costs are

- light with daylight to the extent possible in all allowable spaces such as the lobby, offices with no records use areas, exercise room, break rooms, and restrooms. All light should diffuse and filter UV and IR radiation appropriately to avoid light damage;

- install occupancy sensors, automatic dimmers, automatic blinds, and daylight switches wherever possible to control unnecessary illumination. These work well in areas such as staff restrooms, storage rooms, mechanical and electrical rooms, custodial areas, and loading docks. Daylight harvesting controls switch lighting off or cause lights to dim when daylight is at a certain level;

- use mercury-free compact high efficiency fluorescent lamps with appropriate filtering and bi-level ballasts, instead of incandescent ones. Note: incandescent lamps will be phased out by 2016 and will require heat filters;

- paint the building interior throughout with light colored reflective surfaces to minimize glare and energy use and maximize brightness;

- install manual bi-level switching capacity repository-wide;

- set up operational procedures that maximize cost efficiency. Procedures can include cleaning the light fixtures, training staff to turn off lights when not in use, and reducing after-hours lighting by overlapping staff and maintenance schedules.

The cost efficiencies of using visible light within building interiors, which is known as "daylighting," must be balanced against the need to protect collections from damaging UV and IR light. Choose lamps, windows, and exhibit glass that are fitted with

- UV absorbing acrylic filters (e.g., UF 3 Plexiglas that reduces 95–98% of UV light);

- glass filters;

- dichroic glass filters;

- dimmers (Note: dimmer switches may be inappropriate in such areas as reading rooms, labs, and offices because they may provide uneven illumination.

Incandescent lights should have heat absorbing filters. The minimum distance between the light, particularly incandescent lamps, and the collection item or record should be 20 inches [50 cm].

Fluorescent bulbs may pose some additional costs, such as the need to regularly purchase and replace screens or filters to protect collections from UV and IR. Costs of low UV fluorescent lamps are high, but appear inexpensive when compared to remediation costs when materials are damaged. High-efficiency low UV fluorescent lamps are frequently chosen for archival and special collections buildings.

### 6.1.2 Safety

Most archival materials are highly sensitive to light exposure, capable of being damaged relatively rapidly. The light sensitivity of archival materials mandates the use of lower lighting levels that are a safe distance from collections materials to avoid heat damage. In addition, archives must use less damaging lighting sources and types (non-UV), install special UV screening devices (such as light filters, shades, blinds, and other devices), and provide excellent ventilation and cooling. Manage light damage through prevention by keeping light exposure to a minimum.

The most common problems from light exposure are

- IR radiation heats materials, leading to accelerated aging, embrittlement, and yellowing;
- UV radiation causes disintegration or structural weakness of materials, color shifts in pigments or dyes, and yellowing or darkening of lignins, resins, starches, and glues in collections materials;
- visible light bleaches colors on materials, causing fading, darkening, and yellowing of collections materials, as well as color shifts in dyes and pigments.

The level of damage caused by light depends upon

- length or duration of the exposure;
- intensity of the exposure (light level in foot candles or lux);
- wavelength of light to which the materials are exposed;
- types of materials being exposed.

The longer the exposure, the more intense the light exposure is, the shorter the wavelength, or the more sensitive the material, the greater the damage. Light damage can also be made worse by exposure to other environmental factors such as oxygen, relative humidity, and temperature. Refer to Section 3.

When renovating older buildings, be sure that the lighting systems do not block the sprinkler heads or impact their effectiveness by blocking sprinkler spray. Pay particular attention to fluorescent lighting ballasts, as historically, some ballasts have posed fire risks.

## 6.1.3 Functional

Archivists and designers should determine a space's light levels based upon the functions to occur in the space. Designers may propose the use of light as a design element to add visual interest and drama to a space via skylights, clerestories, chandeliers, specialty lights with dimmer switches, plant lights, embedded LED lighting in auditoriums, spotlights, and exterior spotlights and wall washing lights. While often aesthetically desirable, staff must ensure that the design-based lighting elements do not pose challenges to records preservation, raise ongoing energy costs, pose risks when moving materials into and out of the building, or require substantial additional cooling to control their heat. Examine proposed aesthetic lighting uses closely for their costs and risks to the collections.

Table 6-1 specifies recommended lighting levels for spaces in archival facilities. Sections 6.2 to 6.8 give further explanation regarding lighting guidelines for each of the space types found in archival facilities.

## Table 6-1 Lighting Levels in Foot Candles and Lux

| Space Type | Space Name | Lighting Level in Lux and Foot Candles | Maximum UV Level in Microwatts per Lumen | Notes |
|---|---|---|---|---|
| Stacks | Stacks | 19–46 foot candles [200–500 lux] | 10 | No windows or skylights; UV filters; 20 inches [50 centimeters] between bulb and collections. |
| | Cold Storage | 19–46 foot candles [200–500 lux] | 10 | Thermal tempered lights; UV filters. |
| **Mixed Use** | | | | |
| | Processing Room(s) | 19–46 foot candles [200–500 lux] | 10 | No windows or skylights; UV filters; 20 inches [50 centimeters] between bulb and collections. |
| | Conservation Laboratory—Dry | 19–46 foot candles [200–500 lux] | 10 | Controlled and color balanced light; UV filters; task lighting. |
| | Conservation Laboratory—Wet | 19–46 foot candles [200–500 lux] | 10 | Damp-labeled (DL) or Wet-labeled (WL) fixtures. |
| | Special Media Laboratory | 19–46 foot candles [200–500 lux] | 10 | Controlled and color balanced light; UV filters; task lighting. |
| | Reformatting Lab | 5–139 foot candles [50–1,500 lux] | 10 | Controlled and color balanced light; UV filters; task lighting. |
| | Exhibits | 3–19 foot candles [30–200 lux] | 10 | Most in the 5–9 foot candles [50–100 lux] range; Dimmers and occupancy sensors; fiber optic lighting; 24–36 inches from collections. |
| **Reading Rooms** | | | | |
| | Textual | 19–46 foot candles [200–500 lux] | 10 | Diffuse, color balanced; UV filters; low-level lighting with brighter task lights. |
| | Microfilm | 5–9 foot candles [50–100 lux] | 10 | No windows; UV filters; task lighting |
| | Audiovisual | 19–46 foot candles [200–500 lux] | 10 | Low-level lighting—19–28 foot candles [200–300 lux]; UV filters; lighting zones; task lights. |
| | Records Holding Area | 19–46 foot candles [200–500 lux] | 10 | No windows or skylights; UV filters; 20 inches [50 centimeters] between bulb and collections. |
| | Researcher Registration/ Orientation Consultation | 19–46 foot candles [200–500 lux] | 10 | UV filters; Online registration may require diffuse and lower lighting (5–19 foot candles [50–100 lux]). |
| | Finding Aids Room | 19–46 foot candles [200–500 lux] | 10 | Online catalog searching may require diffuse and lower lighting (5–19 foot candles [50–100 lux]). |

| | | | | |
|---|---|---|---|---|
| **Public Spaces** | | | | |
| | Lobby | 28–46 foot candles [300–500 lux] | 10 | Bright lighting; day lighting and accent lighting. |
| | Lockers/Locker Room | 28–46 foot candles [300–500 lux] | 10 | Occupancy sensors and automatic shut offs. |
| | Auditorium/ Training/ Classroom(s) | 19–46 foot candles [200–500 lux] | 10 | Lighting controls; avoid systems that produce heat or noise. |
| | Meeting Spaces | 19–70 foot candles [200–750 lux] | 10 | 28 foot candles [300 lux] is standard. |
| | Food Service Area | 7–70 foot candles [75–750 lux] | 10 | Kitchens should have 70 foot candles [750 lux]; dining can have day lighting and 7–18.5 foot candles [75–200 lux] |
| | Gift Shop | 70 foot candles [750 lux] | 10 | |
| **Staff Spaces** | | | | |
| | Offices | 28–70 foot candles [300–750 lux] | 10 | |
| | Lunchroom | 7–70 foot candles [75–750 lux] | 10 | Dining can have day lighting and 18.5 foot candles [200 lux] |
| | Lockers/Locker Room | 28–46 foot candles [300–500 lux] | 10 | Occupancy sensors and automatic shut-offs; DL or WL fixtures if needed. |
| **Non-Public Spaces** | | | | |
| | Loading Dock/Receiving | 19–46 foot candles [200–500 lux] | 10 | Recommended are 28 foot candles [300 lux]. |
| | Supply Storage/ Warehouse | 14–46 foot candles [150–500 lux] | 10 | Depends on activity levels. |
| | Computer Room | 19–46 foot candles [200–500 lux] | 10 | No windows or skylights. |
| | Security Office | 19–46 foot candles [200–500 lux] | 10 | May need lighting zones with dimmers and flash capabilities. |
| **General Spaces** | | | | |
| | Restrooms | 28 foot candles [300 lux] | 10 | DL or WL fixtures. |
| | Corridors | 14–28 foot candles [150–300 lux] | 10 | |
| | Stairs | 14–28 foot candles [150–300 lux] | 10 | |
| | Elevators | 14–28 foot candles [150–300 lux] | 10 | |
| | Directional Signage | 19–28 foot candles [200–300 lux] | 10 | |
| | Exterior | 1–19 foot candles [5–200 lux] | | |

## 6.2 STACKS

### 6.2.1 Paper/Films/Electronic Records Stacks

19–46 foot candles [200–500 lux]

Stacks must not have windows, skylights, or clerestories. Existing windows or other natural light sources must be completely blocked.

All light frequencies < 400 nanometers (nm) must be filtered so that 95 to 98% of the UV light is reduced.

The artificial lighting levels should be kept as low as possible in stacks but be bright enough for staff to read container labels. The lighting level should be at least 10 to 15 foot candles [108 to 161 lux] at the floor. In stacks, light levels may vary at different heights. Generally the higher light levels occur at the top the shelves, sometimes leading to uneven fading of collections containers and unboxed materials. The lowest light levels occur at the bottom shelves, sometimes making it difficult to read container labels.

Low IR (heat) lighting should be used in stacks. There should be a 20 inch [50 centimeter] distance between the lighting source and the nearest collection item. Heat from lights can be reduced by increasing the distance of the collections from the lighting source, by using higher ceilings, and by cooling the stack. Ensure that IR shielding is provided to all lighting sources and that all ballasts pose no fire hazard.

Lighting mechanisms must not impede sprinkler effectiveness. In addition, lighting fixtures must not obstruct access to the shelves.

Luminaires can be attached to regular or mobile shelving or may be set up in zones attached to the ceiling. Lighting should be fitted with sensors, occupancy detectors, diffusers, and dimmers to help conserve power and limit the heat and light exposure of the collections. Digital Addressable Lighting Interface (DALI) lighting systems allow hour-by-hour programming of light levels using software and wall controls.

Large stacks may need to be divided into lighting zones. Within zones, position lighting along entryways and aisles to reduce shadows. Lighter floor coverings, those with a Munsell Color System value of not less than 7, provide better reflection, assist in enhancing the lower lighting levels in stack aisles, and make lighting the aisles easier.

Emergency lighting, with a back-up power source, must be continuously available in stacks for emergency egress. In older buildings, until emergency lighting is installed, mount removable motion activated flashlights strategically throughout the stack and mark them with luminescent labels or paint so they are easy to find in an emergency.

## 6.2.2 Cold Storage Stacks

19–46 foot candles [200–500 lux]

Cold storage stacks should use sturdy and well protected thermally-tempered lights. The recessed or metal caged lights should be fitted with UV filters, occupancy detectors, diffusers and dimmers.

Refer to Section 6.2.1 for additional guidelines for stack lighting.

## 6.3 MIXED-USE SPACES

### 6.3.1 Processing Rooms

19–46 foot candles [200–500 lux]

Processing rooms should not have windows, skylights, or clerestories. Existing windows or other natural light sources should be either completely blocked or covered with blackout blinds, shades, or screens with both IR and UV filters.

All light frequencies < 400 nm must be filtered so that 95 to 98% of the UV light is reduced.

Reflective and light colored surfaces will help avoid glare and eye strain. Light at the work tables must have a higher illumination level of at least 46 foot candles [500 lux] and little glare.

While the general lighting level should be between 19 and 46 foot candles [200–500 lux], detailed processing work with faded or difficult to read materials may require brighter lighting up to 139 foot candles [1,500 lux]. Mobile task lighting will bridge this lighting gap, and may include rolling high intensity task lights and lighting panels for negatives, slides, or transparencies.

Use low IR (heat) lighting. Heat from the lights can be reduced by increasing the distance of the collections from the light source and by cooling the room.

Lighting fixtures may be recessed, surface mounted, or hanging. Recessed lighting is preferred as it poses fewer risks when moving oversized materials. The lights should be low emission, low heat, with diffuse and color balanced lighting. Lighting should be fitted with sensors, occupancy detectors, diffusers, and dimmers to help conserve power and limit the heat and light exposure of the collections. Use appropriate emergency lighting.

## 6.3.2 Conservation Laboratory—Dry

19–46 foot candles [200–500 lux]

Conservation labs should not have windows, skylights, or clerestories so that the lighting sources can be tightly controlled, consistent, and color balanced. Existing windows or other natural light sources must be UV filtered and have shades or blinds.

All light frequencies < 400 nm must be filtered so that 95 to 98% of the UV light is reduced.

Conservation labs should have lighting with a color rendering index of 85 or more, and a correlated color temperature of 2,900 to 4,200 Kelvin (K). These labs require moderate levels of diffuse ambient lighting plus powerful and flexible task lighting such as those provided by portable balanced arm lamps. Provide both fluorescent and incandescent lamps and filters that provide lighting levels up to 139 foot candles [1,500 lux]. The highest levels of task lighting should be where examination, treatment, and documentation occur. Luminaires may include a wide variety of recessed, hanging, task, and mobile lighting sources.

Conservation and research and testing labs may use equipment that features specialty gamma, IR, laser, UV and X-ray radiation sources that require special shielding or chambers.

Conservation labs should have lighting zones for such activities as examination, special instrumentation, oversized collections, chemical and biological fume hoods, wet spaces, and photographic areas. Some of these tasks may require ground fault interrupters and specially tempered glass luminaires.

### 6.3.3 Conservation Laboratory—Wet

19–46 foot candles [200–500 lux]

Wet labs should use Damp-Labeled (DL) fixtures. If the humidity will be extremely high, then Wet-Labeled (WL) fixtures should be used.

Refer to section 6.3.2 for additional guidelines for conservation lab lighting.

### 6.3.4 Special Media Laboratory

19–46 foot candles [200–500 lux]

Special media labs should not have windows, skylights, or clerestories so that the lighting sources can be tightly controlled, consistent, and color balanced. Existing windows or other natural light sources must be UV filtered and have shades or blinds.

All light frequencies < 400 nm must be filtered so that 95 to 98% of the UV light is reduced.

Special media labs should have lighting with a color rendering index of 85 or more, and a correlated color temperature of 2,900 to 4,200 K. These labs require moderate levels of diffuse ambient lighting plus powerful and flexible task lighting such as those provided by portable balanced arm lamps. Provide both fluorescent and incandescent lamps and filters that provide lighting levels up to 139 foot candles [1,500 lux]. The highest levels of task lighting should be where examination, treatment, and documentation occur. Luminaires may include a wide variety of recessed, hanging, task and mobile lighting sources.

These labs should have lighting zones for such activities as examination, oversized collections, reformatting, and photographic areas. Some of these tasks may require ground fault interrupters and specially tempered glass luminaires.

### 6.3.5 Reformatting Laboratory

5–139 foot candles [50–1,500 lux]

Lighting levels can be as low as 5 foot candles [50 lux] or as high as 139 foot candles [1,500 lux] depending on the required tasks and treatments.

Refer to Section 6.3.4 for additional guidelines for reformatting lab lighting.

### 6.3.6 Exhibits

3–19 foot candles [30–200 lux]

Exhibit areas should not have windows, skylights, or clerestories. Natural light must never be used to illuminate exhibits. Existing windows or other natural light sources must be UV filtered and have shades or blinds.

All light frequencies < 400 nm must be filtered so that 95 to 98% of the UV light is reduced.

Exhibit lighting levels must balance the preservation needs of the collections with the viewing needs of the visitors. Most of the exhibition area is lighted in the range of 5 to 9 foot candles [50 to 100 lux]. In exhibition lighting, the lower the lighting level and the shorter the duration, the lower the damage will be to the material. Human eyes can adapt to viewing materials in low light situations. A minimum of 3 foot candles [30 lux] is required for human color perception. A maximum of 5 foot candles [50 lux] protects light sensitive materials.

The lighting system must not heat up the collections:

- A minimum distance of 24 inches [61 centimeters] is required between the lighting and collections when fluorescent lights are used.

- A minimum of 36 inches [91 centimeters] is required between the lighting and collections when incandescent lights are used.

Exhibit lighting should have a color temperature of 3,500 K and white light should be used.

Exhibit lighting should be off when the exhibit is not being viewed either through computerized lighting or a master switch. Use dimmers and occupancy sensors.

Fiber optic lighting should be used for new exhibit cases and major renovations. If fluorescent or incandescent lighting is used in exhibit areas, the lights must be kept outside the exhibit case and must be filtered to <400 nm. If external case lighting is not possible, the lighting should be in a separate chamber of the case with full venting, heat filters, and a heat dissipating fan.

Historical case lighting tends to be incandescent, which will be phased out of production by 2016. Historical cabinet lighting is compact fluorescent, while under-shelf lighting is tungsten, halogen, or metal halide. Often this historical lighting is hardwired, small, customizable in length, and with the electrical elements and heat source located outside the case. If electrical or heat sources are inside the exhibit case, display only copies of archival collections. Buy new cases or rewire old cases before exhibiting original materials.

## 6.4  READING ROOM(S)

Reading rooms should not have skylights or light wells to limit possibilities of leakage and to limit light damage. Windows and other natural light sources must be UV filtered and have flexible use shades or screens with both IR and UV filters.

### 6.4.1  Textual Reading Room

19–46 foot candles [200–500 lux]

All light frequencies < 400 nm must be filtered so that 95 to 98% of the UV light is reduced.

Reflective and light colored surfaces will help avoid glare and eye strain. Ambient overhead lights should be diffuse, color balanced, and the relatively low level of 14 to 28 foot candles [150 to 300 lux]. Supplement ambient lighting with mobile task lighting up to 70 foot candles [750 lux] at reading room tables.

Use low IR (heat) lighting such as fluorescents. As incandescent lighting is being phased out, use energy efficient low UV fluorescents with low ballast factor ballasts.

Reduce heat from the lights by providing ceiling heights of 10 feet [3 meters] or higher and by cooling the room. Keep lights off when the room is not in use. Use occupancy sensors and automatic shut-offs.

Use appropriate emergency lighting.

### 6.4.2 Microfilm Reading Room

5–9 foot candles [50–100 lux]

Microfilm reading rooms should not have windows or existing windows should be covered. Provide point-of-use local task lighting for machine users.

Refer to Section 6.4 for additional guidelines for reading room lighting.

### 6.4.3 Audiovisual Reading Room

19–46 foot candles [200–500 lux]

Preferred lighting level is 19 to 28 foot candles [200 to 300 lux]. Use lighting zones for different types of research, including light tables, TV monitors, computer monitors, and desktop research.

Refer to Section 6.4 for additional guidelines for reading room lighting.

### 6.4.4 Records Holding Area

19–46 foot candles [200–500 lux]

Records holding areas should not have windows, skylights, or clerestories. Existing windows or other natural light sources should be either completely blocked or covered with blackout blinds, shades, or screens with both IR and UV filters.

All light frequencies < 400 nm must be filtered so that 95 to 98% of the UV light is reduced.

Use low IR (heat) lighting. Heat from the lights can be reduced by increasing the distance of the collections from the light source and by cooling the room.

Lighting fixtures may be recessed, surface mounted or hanging. Recessed lighting is preferred as it poses fewer risks when moving oversized materials. The lights should be low emission, low heat, with diffuse and color balanced lighting. Lighting should be fitted with sensors, occupancy detectors, diffusers, and dimmers to help conserve power and limit the heat and light exposure of the collections. Use appropriate emergency lighting.

Refer to Section 6.3.1 for additional lighting guidelines.

### 6.4.5 Researcher Registration/Orientation/Consultation

19–46 foot candles [200–500 lux]

Spaces where computer monitors or microfilm readers/printers are used may require more diffuse and lower lighting, such as 5 to 19 foot candles [50 to 100 lux].

Use down lighting or side lighting to illuminate pamphlet or handout racks.

If camera set-ups are required for badge photography, use lighting zones set up with dimmers and flash capabilities.

### 6.4.6 Finding Aids Room

19–46 foot candles [200–500 lux]

Spaces where computer monitors or microfilm readers/printers are used may require more diffuse and lower lighting, such as 5 to 19 foot candles [50 to 100 lux].

## 6.5 PUBLIC SPACES

### 6.5.1 Lobby

28–46 foot candles [300–500 lux]

Lobbies are generally bright spaces of at least 28 foot candles [300 lux]; this helps the eyes adjust from the bright outside light. Often windows make up 5 to 10% of the floor area of the lobby. Lobby lighting also may include more dramatic accent lighting such as light wells, skylights, and wall washers. None of these features should be located directly above stacks.

### 6.5.2 Lockers/Locker Room

28–46 foot candles [300–500 lux]

The Illuminating Engineering Society of North America (IESNA) cites 28 foot candles [300 lux] as the standard lighting level for locker rooms.

Lighting should be controlled by occupancy sensors, preferably ultrasonic sensors, and automatic shut-offs. However, at least 20% of the lights should be zoned separately and be left on during building access hours. Consider light diffusers and/or bouncing light off of the ceiling.

Use DL or WL fixtures if sinks and showers are located in the locker room.

### 6.5.3 Auditorium/Training/Classroom(s)

19–46 foot candles [200–500 lux]

If the space has windows, they should be fully filtered and have shades, blinds, or curtains to limit outside lights during audiovisual presentations.

Provide lighting controls. Light sensors and dimmers are required to bring down lighting levels to 5 foot candles [50 lux] for audiovisual presentations. Consider DALI lighting, which uses programmable software and wall controls.

Projection rooms should have manual and programmable lighting controls.

Avoid using any lighting systems that produce noise or heat.

### 6.5.4 Meeting Spaces

19–70 foot candles [200–750 lux]

IESNA cites 28 foot candles [300 lux] as the standard lighting level for meeting rooms.

Provide higher levels of illumination of 70 foot candles [750 lux] at the desk top level. Use light colored paint and light colored surfaces to reduce eye strain.

Meeting rooms should have occupancy sensors and automatic shut-offs. Consider light diffusers and/or bouncing light off of the ceiling. Provide lighting level controls.

### 6.5.5 Food Service Area

7–70 foot candles [75–750 lux]

Kitchens should have 70 foot candles [750 lux].

Dining areas should have a minimum of 7 foot candles [75 lux]. Daylighting is often used as a partial lighting source and there is evidence that it enhances the mood of diners.

Combined spaces should have 19 foot candles [200 lux].

### 6.5.6 Gift Shop

70 foot candles [750 lux]

IESNA cites 70 foot candles [750 lux] as the standard for gift shops.

## 6.6 STAFF SPACES

### 6.6.1 Offices

28–70 foot candles [300–750 lux]

IESNA cites 70 foot candles [750 lux] for offices where reading and writing occur. Generally windows are 5 to 10% of the floor area for ambient lighting.

### 6.6.2 Lunchroom

7–70 foot candles [75–750 lux] See Section 6.5.5.

### 6.6.3 Lockers/Locker Room

28–46 foot candles [300–500 lux]

See Section 6.5.2.

## 6.7 NON-PUBLIC SPACES

### 6.7.1 Loading Dock/Receiving

14–37 foot candles [150–400 lux]

IESNA recommends 28 foot candles [300 lux] to aid loading and unloading vehicles. Perimeter areas near the loading dock can have lower lighting levels at 14 to 19 foot candles [150 to 200 lux].

### 6.7.2 Supply Storage/Warehouse

14–46 foot candles [150–500 lux]

IESNA cites that warehouse lighting depends on the activity levels.

- Low activity: 7 foot candles [75 lux]
- Medium activity: 14 foot candles [150 lux]
- High activity: 28 foot candles [300 lux]

### 6.7.3 Computer Room

19–46 foot candles [200–500 lux]

Computer rooms should not have skylights or light wells to limit possibilities of leakage and to limit light damage.

### 6.7.4 Security Office

19–46 foot candles [200–500 lux]

If camera set-ups are required for badge photography, use lighting zones set up with dimmers and flash capabilities.

## 6.8 GENERAL SPACES

### 6.8.1 Restrooms

28 foot candles [300 lux]

IESNA cites 28 foot candles [300 lux] for restrooms. Strong lighting in restrooms provides assistance in grooming and a sense of security.

Sinks and mirrors should be lit from above and from the side. Restrooms also benefit from light colored finishes, high color rendering (Color Rendering Index 80+), and the introduction of daylight through filtered translucent glass blocks or other obscured glass.

Restrooms should have DL fixtures. If the humidity will be extremely high, then WL fixtures should be used.

Lighting should be controlled by occupancy sensors, preferably ultrasonic sensors, and automatic shut-offs. However, at least 20% of the lights should be zoned separately and be left on during building access hours.

### 6.8.2 Corridors

14–28 foot candles [150–300 lux]

IESNA cites 14 foot candles [150 lux] for corridors.

Corridors may feature wall washing lights, indirect lighting such as 4 feet [120 cm] long T-8 fluorescents, or compact fluorescent lights. These lights do not require special filtration unless the space includes exhibitions.

Corridors are excellent places for light wells, spotlights to highlight wall art, and other design lighting as long as they are not directly over stacks, processing, or reading rooms.

### 6.8.3 Stairs/Elevators

14–28 foot candles [150–300 lux]

IESNA cites 14 foot candles [150 lux] for elevators. Elevators may feature wall washing lights, indirect lighting, such as 4 feet [1.2 meters] long T-8 fluorescents, or compact fluorescent lights.

### 6.8.4 Directional Signage

19–28 foot candles [200–300 lux]

### 6.8.5 Exterior

1–19 foot candles [5–200 lux]

Exterior lighting should appropriately illuminate the building entrances, loading docks, parking spaces, pathways, sidewalks, and perimeters. IESNA cites 1 foot candle [15 lux] for street lighting.

- Entrances: Light building entrances for humans and cars at the 14 to 19 foot candle [150 to 200 lux] level.

- Pathways: 5 to 9 foot candles [50 to 100 lux].

- Perimeter lighting should be overlapping, continuous, even (without hot or cold spots), and available on both sides of the perimeter barriers. Tempered lighting fixtures protected by wire cages or other covers may be necessary.

Section 7

# MATERIALS AND FINISHES

*Michele F. Pacifico*

7.1 **RATIONALE**

Archival materials are fragile and are subject to chemical, biological, and physical damage. Deterioration of collections is hastened when the records are stored and used in unsuitable environments. In addition to proper climate and filtration conditions, archival collections require storage environments that are constructed with materials and finishes that minimize the off-gassing of volatile organic compounds (VOC) and other chemicals that can contaminate the air and degrade the records. Materials that contain biological contaminants or might invite mold are also to be avoided in records storage environments. All materials and finishes used in archival facilities must meet the requirements of the building life safety and fire codes. Furthermore, because archival facilities are usually constructed to last decades, if not centuries, the materials and finishes selected should be of the highest quality, extremely durable, and attractive.

Avoiding materials that cause significant off-gassing should be a major consideration when carrying out building planning, especially for stacks. Off-gassing of harmful substances should be minimized in the areas where records are used, including processing areas, exhibit areas, laboratories, and reading rooms. In reality, most adhesives and coatings do not dry, or cure, instantaneously; moreover, nearly all give off some gas or vapor while curing. The goal for selecting materials and finishes for archival facilities is to avoid those that are unstable or slow curing.

As much as possible, paints, sealants, caulks, wood products, foams, and other materials selected for archival facilities should have low or no VOC emissions.

### 7.1.1 Prohibited Materials

Certain materials must be prohibited from archival stacks and exhibit cases where original documents are displayed. Prohibited materials should be avoided in processing rooms, records holding areas, laboratories, and exhibit galleries. Materials and finishes deemed "prohibited" have been identified by conservators, chemists, and archivists as such because of their deleterious properties that are known to rapidly degrade records. Prohibited materials include

- asbestos;
- cellulose nitrate;
- lacquers and adhesives;
- acid-curing silicone sealants and adhesives;
- sulfur containing materials;
- pressure sensitive adhesives;
- formaldehyde;
- unstable chlorine polymers (PVC).

See Appendix A for a list of prohibited materials for archival facilities. It should be noted that some materials listed as prohibited are currently unavoidable in some building materials but every attempt should be made to substitute safer materials as they become available. For example, electrical cables contain PVC, a prohibited material on the list.

### 7.1.2 Selection and Testing

Within the last twenty years, a good deal of information has been developed about the use of materials and finishes in archival facilities. Archives, museums, conservation laboratories, and related industries shared information about dangerous or questionable building materials through technical publications and their websites. These resources are cited in the Bibliography. In addition, the National Archives and Records Administration (NARA) outlines test methods for certain products in the specifications for their archival facilities. For example, NARA has standard test methods for painted or powder coated finished metal surfaces. A list of the products that have been tested by NARA's Research and Testing Lab, such as tapes, inks, and boxes, is published on its website, http://www.archives.gov.

Unfortunately, it is not possible to identify all of the materials and products that should be avoided or used in archival facilities and even tested materials change formulas and ingredients and must be repeatedly checked and monitored. Continual evaluation and testing is needed as new and reformulated products are proposed for the archival facilities. Institutions that are considering using new or untested products in areas where records are stored, exhibited, or used should review the Material Safety Data Sheets (MSDS) for these products. One place to start is checking the items against those substances listed on the Prohibited Materials list in Appendix A or discussed in these guidelines. Further consultation with certified laboratories, conservators, chemists, and experts in this field should be considered, especially for new products to be used in stacks.

## 7.2 EXTERNAL BUILDING MATERIALS

The external building materials for an archives facility should ensure the permanence of the records and meet the storage and public demands of the building. Materials must be durable, provide appropriate protection from heat, cold, humidity, and moisture, be easy to maintain and keep clean, and meet the facility's program requirements. Whenever possible, the external building materials should be limited to those known to be stable and inert, and that will minimize the emission of harmful substances such as smoke and soot in the event of a fire. Particular attention should be paid to insulation, adhesives, epoxy materials, and caulks. All exposed concrete slabs, including spaces beneath raised floor systems, should be sealed or coated to prevent moisture migration and dust. Refer to Section 2 for building construction guidelines and Section 7.3.1a for information on sealants and coatings for concrete.

### 7.2.1 Building Acclimatization

In newly constructed or renovated facilities, time should be allotted for the building materials to dry or cure before staff or collections move into the building. This allows the internal environments to stabilize before any archival records move into the building. A minimum of four weeks is recommended to acclimatize an area within the building, although a longer time period is better for the stacks. All building air handlers should be in continuous exhaust mode during the acclimatization period to reduce the level of pollutants. Air filters should be changed before archival material is moved into the building.

## 7.3 STACKS

The stacks should maintain the highest level of cleanliness and environmental controls in the archival facility. Records will spend more than 90% of their time in the stacks and high quality storage is the best investment that archives can make. Materials and finishes that must be prohibited in stacks are listed in Appendix A. Refer to Section 3 for acceptable levels of pertinent gases and particulates.

Stacks must be limited to the storage of the archival collections. Consequently, they should incorporate only the materials necessary to house and store the collections. Materials typically used in stacks include shelving; cabinets; boxes or containers housing the collections; and mechanical lifts, book trucks, and carts used to move and transport records. Staff workstations, copiers, and other equipment must never be located in stacks.

### 7.3.1 Floors

The floors of the stacks need to be extremely durable, level, free from dust, and have a smooth finish allowing book trucks and carts to be easily maneuvered by staff.

**Table 7-1 Stack Floor Materials**

| Floor Material | Recommended | Not Recommended |
|---|---|---|
| Concrete | x | |
| Wood | | x |
| Bamboo | | x |
| Carpet | | x |
| Tile | | x |
| Cork Products | | x |

Recommended:

a. *Concrete*

Sealed and epoxy covered concrete is the recommended flooring for stacks. Concrete is an economical and durable floor solution that if properly sealed meets the criteria for a safe and inert material. The concrete floors should first be sealed with a low volatile organic compound acrylic membrane curing compound. The sealer is then topped with an application of a floor epoxy. The epoxy coating should meet the guidelines established for paint and finishes with respect to off-gassing of VOC and other gases. Bare concrete floors should be avoided because they will introduce fine particulate, alkaline dust into the stack environment. Current guidelines specify that the VOC off-gassing of any epoxy and floor coatings be limited by restricting the use of toluene and xylene in the floor coating mix to less than 0.1 parts per million.

The following products must not be used in concrete floor coatings:

- Biocide
- Formaldehyde
- Acetic acid
- Amine-based products

**Not Recommended:**

b. *Wood*

Wood floors are not recommended for stacks. Wood floors are rarely strong enough to support archival collections and are combustible. In addition, wood floats in water and does not hold if it gets water damaged. Wood is food to some insects and animals and will attract common pests such as termites and vermin.

All woods, even old and well seasoned woods, generate volatile acids. Oak, frequently found in older buildings, is the most acidic wood and potentially the most dangerous—the main VOC released is acetic acid. Cedar is also highly acidic. The acids in raw woods will cause staining to collections and containers. Plywood and other wood composites are even more problematic than solid wood because they may be fabricated with adhesives or resins containing formaldehyde, which oxidizes to formic acid, and off-gas unacceptable amounts of other pollutants. If plywood is used in stacks, exterior grade plywood bonded with exterior glue is recommended with additional seals applied to the wood.

Additional measures should be taken to limit the acidic off-gassing if wood products are present. However, no coating or sealant can completely block the emission of VOC for prolonged periods of time. Choose a sealant that does not give off problematic volatiles of its own. In general, avoid oil-based products. Coatings generally considered safe are moisture-borne polyurethanes and two-part epoxy sealants. Not all polyurethanes are safe, however, and new products should be tested. Paints can also be used to seal wood. Oil-based paints and stains should be avoided. Two-part epoxy paints create a good barrier while latex and acrylic is a less effective barrier to off-gassing.

Any sealant or finish applied to wood floors should attempt to limit the off-gassing of formaldehyde to no more than 4 parts per billion or 5 micrograms per cubic meter and limit the total volatile organic compounds off-gassed to not exceed 100 micrograms per square meter. See Table 3-2 for off-gassing limits for gaseous contaminates.

### c. *Bamboo*

Bamboo flooring generates volatile acids and is not recommended for stacks. Almost all bamboo floors have formaldehyde binders. In addition, bamboo is combustible. It is a soft flooring and rarely strong enough to support archival collections.

### d. *Carpet*

Carpets off-gas harmful solvents and are combustible and should not be used in stacks. They trap dust and are more difficult to keep clean in a stack environment than bare floors. They can also trap moisture and present mold problems. In addition, it is difficult to maneuver lifts and book trucks on a carpeted surface.

### e. *Tile*

Ceramic and stone tiles must be adhered to the floor with grouts and adhesives that may off-gas harmful solvents and should not be used in stacks. In addition, they do not stand up well to heavy lift and book truck traffic. Vinyl is prohibited and the glues used in vinyl tiles have traditionally been very detrimental to records. If used, select those where the off-gassing of formaldehyde is no more than 4 parts per billion or 5 micrograms per cubic meter and where the total volatile organic compounds off-gassed from the tiles and adhesives does not exceed 100 micrograms per square meter. See Table 3-2.

### f. *Cork and other cork-based products like Marmoleum*

While natural cork does not off-gas VOC, the use of cork flooring products are not recommended for stacks. Cork flooring is often adhered with adhesives and comes with problematic protective coatings. Some products are composites and are combined with PVC backing. Cork flooring can chip, flake, and leave dust. If used, select adhesives where the off-gassing of formaldehyde is no more than 4 parts per billion or 5 micrograms per cubic meter and where the total volatile organic compounds off-gassed from the tiles and adhesives does not exceed 100 micrograms per square meter. See Table 3-2.

102    *Archival and Special Collections Facilities*

## 7.3.2 Walls, Ceilings, and Exposed Pipes

**Recommended:**

a. *Latex-based paints*

Latex-based paints are recommended for the walls, ceilings and exposed pipes in stacks. If concrete block walls are used in the stacks, they should be primed and painted with latex-based paint to prevent dust. Ceiling pipes and metal wall panels should be coated with an acrylic primer (water reducible) and covered with latex paint.

**Not Recommended:**

b. *Oil-based or alkyd paints*

The use of oil-based and alkyd paints has been proven to be harmful to all media types of archival records and must not be used in stacks.

c. *Drop or suspended ceilings*

Drop or suspended ceilings should be avoided in stacks for reasons of fire safety, dust control, and undetected water leaks and infestation. Drop ceilings inhibit airflow between heated space and the ceiling risking frozen pipes. Drop ceilings are often manufactured of materials that are not safe for archival records. If their use is unavoidable, they should be constructed of materials where the off-gassing of formaldehyde is no more than 4 parts per billion or 5 micrograms per cubic meter and where the total volatile organic compounds off-gassed from the tiles and adhesives does not exceed 100 micrograms per square meter. See Table 3-2.

In addition, routine inspections should be scheduled as part of housekeeping plan. Installion of sticky trays, water alarms, and/or Preservation Environmental Monitors (PEM) are recommended as further precautions if these ceilings are used in stacks.

## 7.3.3 Insulation

**Recommended:**

a. There are a variety of insulation materials available and the choices keep changing. Before selecting insulation, review the

MSDS and eliminate those insulations with formaldehyde or other chemicals that are known to be risky to archival records. In all cases, insulation should not be left exposed. When possible, insulation should be located on the external side of the roof slab and sandwiched between masonry on exterior walls.

**Recommended with Reservations:**

b. *Fiberglass insulation*

Fiberglass insulation, if not well designed and properly installed, poses risks to archival collections and employees. There are many different types of fiberglass products available. Semi-rigid and rigid fiberglass insulations are preferred as they are more durable and the fiberglass will not shed or "rain down" on collections in cases of poor construction or emergencies. Blanket-type fiberglass insulation is not recommended for archival facilities.

**Not Recommended:**

c. *Formaldehyde-based insulation*

d. *Foam-in-place insulation*

e. *Asbestos*

### 7.3.4 Caulks

Caulks are generally used throughout buildings to seal surfaces. There is both a large variety of caulks in use and there is a large diversity of cure products associated with caulks. The best choice is a caulk with no curing byproducts, but these are rare. When selecting caulks for the stacks, care should be taken to select a caulk that will do the least damage to the records. When possible, avoid caulks that release gases that appear on the prohibited list of materials. If possible, have the caulks applied off-site, prior to installation in the stacks, which will allow harmful solvents to off-gas before exposure to the records. In addition, use the mitigation strategies suggested in Section 7.8.

**Table 7-2 Stack Furnishings**

| Material | Recommended | Recommended with Reservations | Not Recommended |
|---|---|---|---|
| Steel | x | | |
| Chrome-Plated Steel | x | | |
| Anodized Aluminum | | x | |
| Wood | | | x |
| Carpet | | | x |
| Fabrics | | | x |

## 7.3.5 Shelving, Cabinet Materials and Storage Furnishings Used in Stacks

Recommended:

a. *Steel*

Steel shelving is the most common shelving and cabinet material used in archival facilities. It is inert and it is not combustible. In the past, baked enamel shelving was commonly used. However, baked enamel off-gases harmful VOC. Steel shelving and cabinets in records storage areas should use a powder coated finish as described in Section 7.3.6.

b. *Chrome-plated steel shelving*

Open chrome-plated stainless-steel wire racks are recommended for boxed material housed in cold storage areas, usually those with temperatures less than 50°F [10°C]. The chrome shelving provides good air circulation and prevents condensation from settling on the containers. The material housed on this kind of shelving must be stored in containers.

Recommended with Reservations:

c. *Anodized aluminum*

Uncoated anodized aluminum is extremely strong yet light in weight. The metal is believed to be nonreactive and without a coating so there are no off-gassing problems. However, aluminum is chemically reactive to acids and some metals such as copper. It may develop rust if there is condensation in the stacks. Aluminum shelves are often pierced, which provides little protection from leaks but provides air flow if needed. It is currently one of the more expensive products on the market for shelving use.

**Not Recommended:**

d. *Wood*

Solid wood and composite wood products are not recommended for use in stacks. Wood generates VOC and is combustible. If presented with wood shelving in records storage areas, the wood should be treated with the appropriate sealant, avoiding all oil-based products as outlined in Section 7.4.3. The shelves should be lined with museum board, polyester film, glass, Plexiglas, or an inert metallic laminate material to prevent collections materials from coming into direct contact with the wood surface. If records must be stored in closed wooden cabinets, the cabinets should be aired out several times a year to minimize the buildup of damaging fumes. Refer to Section 8 for further details on shelving and storage equipment.

e. *Carpet and fabrics*

Carpet and fabrics are not recommended for stacks. Decorative shelving end panels made of carpet, fabric, or laminates should be avoided. All shelving end panels should be made of the same metal and with the same finish as the shelving.

**Other Materials**

Some of the materials used by shelving and cabinet manufacturers may not be suitable for use in stacks. Care must be taken in selecting the plastics, rubbers, caulks, lubricants, adhesives, and other components of the shelving and cabinets.

- *Bumpers*:
  **Recommended:** An acceptable neoprene material.

- *Gaskets*:
  **Recommended:** Acrylic or Teflon.
  **Not Recommended:** Rubber.

- *Sign holders*:
  Recommended: Uncoated aluminum or metal that is painted with acceptable epoxy hybrid paint (see Section 7.3.6).
  Not Recommended: Plastic.

- *High density mobile storage system:*
  Not Recommended: Petroleum, lubricants, and silicones unless sealed within the equipment.

- *Map case drawer cover:*
  Recommended: Polyester.
  Not Recommended: Vinyl.

- *Map case ball bearings:*
  Recommended: Stainless steel.
  Not Recommended: Plastic.

## 7.3.6 Shelving, Cabinet, and Cart Finishes

Most metal storage furniture has a coated surface. The finish should be smooth, nonabrasive, free of irregularities and resistant to chipping. Exposed steel is susceptible to rust and will stain collections.

Recommended:

a. *Electrostatically applied powder coating*

The most recent tests show that electrostatically applied powder coating systems eliminate the greatest potential hazards to archival records. Such processes use a dry system that does not require organic solvents or drying oils for processing the finish. The powder-coating polymer should be a polyester epoxy hybrid or the best equivalent available that does not exceed the off-gassing limits specified in Table 3-2.

Not Recommended:

b. *Baked enamel finish*

Baked enamel off-gases harmful solvents to archival records.

## 7.3.7 Lighting Fixtures

Recommended:

a. *Bare aluminum*

b. *Bare stainless steel*

c. *Powder-coated metal*: metal coated with an electrostatically applied powder coating like that used on the shelving. Refer to Section 7.3.6.

### 7.3.8 Fire Extinguishers

Recommended: Stainless steel.

Not Recommended: Enamel painted extinguishers (usually red or white in color).

### 7.4 PROCESSING AREAS, EXHIBIT GALLERIES, HOLDING AREAS, AND OTHER AREAS WHERE ARCHIVAL COLLECTIONS ARE TEMPORARILY STORED, PROCESSED, OR DISPLAYED

Processing areas, exhibit galleries, and records holding areas will be occupied by staff and temporarily by archival collections. Floor materials and finishes should be durable, attractive, and easy to clean and maintain. As much as possible, care should be taken to develop an environment that is identical to the stacks. The prohibited materials and finishes listed in Appendix A should be avoided in areas where records are used, exhibited, and processed.

Table 7-3 Floor Materials—Temporary Records Storage Areas

| Material | Recommended | Recommended with Reservations | Not Recommended |
|---|---|---|---|
| Concrete | x | | |
| Carpet | | x | |
| Wood | | | x |
| Bamboo | | | x |
| Tile | | | x |
| Cork Products | | | x |

## 7.4.1 Floors

Records will be transported to these areas by some type of wheeled book truck or cart and the floor material selected must be flat and level enough for the carts for a smooth ride. Floors need to be durable, level, easy to clean, and dust free.

Recommended:

a. *Concrete*

Sealed and epoxy covered concrete as described for use in stacks in Section 7.3.1 is the recommended flooring for records use areas because of its fire resistant and inert qualities. However, because these areas are populated by working staff, warmer and more sound absorbent floor coverings are often specified for these spaces. In older buildings the structure may dictate the kind of floor covering that must be used in these spaces.

Acceptable:

b. *Carpet*

Low pile carpet or carpet tiles are acceptable for use in processing rooms or exhibit galleries. Low or no VOC products that meet the Carpet and Rug Institute's Indoor Air Quality Standards (Green Label Program) should be specified. The carpet adhesive should be non-wet adhesive, micro-encapsulated tackifier impregnated into cushion backing solvent-free adhesive (as recommended by manufacturer) for interior installation of vinyl backed carpet. Acrylic-based adhesive must be nonflammable, water-based, and alkali-resistant, mildew-resistant, freeze-thaw stable. Adhesive should release from substrate without leaving residue.

Not Recommended:

c. *Wood*

Solid wood and composite wood floors are not recommended for use in processing areas, exhibit galleries, and holding areas. Follow the guidelines in Section 7.3.1.

d. *Bamboo*

Bamboo floors are not recommended for use in processing areas, exhibit galleries, and holding areas. Follow the guidelines in Section 7.3.1.

e. *Tile*

Although not recommended for processing or exhibit areas, if tile is used the off-gassing of formaldehyde should be no more than 4 parts per billion [5 micrograms per cubic meter]. Select tiles where the total volatile organic compounds off-gassed from the tiles and adhesives does not exceed 100 micrograms per square meter. See Table 3-2.

f. *Cork and other cork-based products like Marmoleum*

While natural cork does not off-gas VOC, the use of cork flooring products are not recommended for use in processing areas, exhibit galleries, and hold areas. Refer to Section 7.3.1.

### 7.4.2 Walls, Ceilings, and Exposed Pipes

Recommended: Latex-based paints.

Not Recommended: Oil-based or alkyd paints.

**Table 7-4 Furniture—Temporary Records Storage Areas**

| Material | Recommended | Recommended with Reservations | Not Recommended |
| --- | --- | --- | --- |
| Metal | x | | |
| Anodized Aluminum | | x | |
| Acrylic | | x | |
| Glass | | x | |
| Solid Wood | | | x |
| Composite Wood | | | x |

### 7.4.3 Furniture

Recommended:

a. *Metal*

Metal shelving and furniture, finished with an electrostatically applied powder coating is recommended for use in processing and records holding areas. Galvanized aluminum and stainless steel also are appropriate materials for furniture in the processing area.

Recommended with Reservations:

b. *Anodized aluminum*

Uncoated anodized aluminum is extremely strong yet light in weight. The metal is believed to be non-reactive and without a coating so there are no off-gassing problems. However, aluminum is chemically reactive to acids and some metals such as copper. It may develop rust if there is condensation. It is currently one of the more expensive products on the market for shelving use.

c. *Acrylic*

In many cases this may not be a practical choice because it is not particularly strong and it is susceptible to scratches.

d. *Glass*

Chipped glass on a table could damage records.

Not Recommended:

e. *Solid wood*

Solid wood furniture is not recommended for use in processing rooms, exhibit galleries, and holding areas for the same reasons discussed in stacks. All woods, even old and well seasoned woods, generate volatile acids and are combustible. Additional measures should be taken to limit the off-gassing if wood products are present. However, no coating or sealant can completely block the emission of VOC for prolonged periods of time. Choose a sealant that does not give off problematic volatiles of its own. In general, avoid oil-based products. Coatings generally considered safe are moisture-borne polyurethanes and two-part epoxy sealants. Not all polyurethanes are safe, however, and new products should be tested. Paints can also be used to seal wood. Oil-based paints and stains should be avoided. Two-part epoxy paints create a good barrier while latex and acrylic barriers for a less effective barrier. Select sealants that limit the off-gassing of formaldehyde to no more than 4 parts per billion [5 micrograms per cubic meter]. Select those where the total volatile organic compounds off-gassed does not exceed 100 micrograms per square meter. See Table 3-2.

### f. *Composite Wood*

Plywood and other wood composites used to make furniture are even more problematic than solid wood. In addition to the organic acids from the wood, the adhesives or resins can emit dangerous levels of formaldehyde, which oxidizes to formic acid. There is little control over the type of wood used in commercial plywood products.

If plywood is used in a processing room, gallery, or holding area, acceptable products are:

- exterior grade plywood bonded with exterior glue;
- overlaid plywood such as plywood with phenol formaldehyde impregnated paper overlays;
- plastic-laminated panels, such as plywood with phenoic laminates (e.g., Formica).

Wood panel products to be avoided include

- interior plywood;
- interior particleboard;
- wafer board;
- chipboard;
- untempered hardboard;
- oil tempered hardboard;
- fiberboard.

The safer adhesives for use in wood panel products include

- phenol formaldehyde;
- polyurea;
- epoxy.

Avoid the following adhesives:

- urea formaldehyde
- polyformaldehyde
- drying oil
- rubber contact cement.

g. *Wood shelving*

If presented with wood shelving in processing areas, the wood should be treated with the appropriate sealant. In addition, the shelves can be lined with museum board, polyester film, glass, Plexiglas, or an inert metallic laminate material to prevent collection materials from coming into direct contact with the wood. If collections must be stored in closed wooden cabinets, drill holes to provide air circulation and air out the cabinets several times a year to minimize buildup of damaging fumes.

## 7.4.4 Fabrics

Fabrics used in processing rooms, exhibit galleries, and other like areas should be chemically stable. Refer to Section 7.5.1 for specific fabrics to avoid in areas where archival collections are used or stored.

## 7.5 EXHIBIT CASES

Exhibit cases can be built in or stand-alone units in an archival facility. Exhibit cases, especially those that display archival records, should be specified as carefully as the stacks materials described in Section 7.3. Materials and finishes that should never be used in exhibit cases are listed in Appendix A. Exhibit cases displaying original documents should be aerated for a minimum of four weeks prior to the installation of the archival records.

**Recommended:**

a. *Stainless steel*

b. *Aluminum metal panels*

c. *Acid-free paper honeycomb panels*

d. *High-density polyethylene*

e. *Aluminum/polyethylene laminates*

f. *Glass*

g. *Polyester sheets*

h. *Polypropylene sheets*

**Not Recommended:**

i. *Wood*

The use of wood or wood products should be avoided in the construction of exhibit cases. If wood must be used, choose a type that is low in harmful emissions and seal the wood with the appropriate sealants as discussed in Section 7.4.3. If wood is used when displaying documents, the wood should be isolated from the collection materials using a vapor barrier such as aluminum foil, a safe paint or varnish, or other appropriate barrier material.

### 7.5.1 Fabric

Select fabric linings for exhibit cases with care. All fabrics should be washed to remove any sizing. Fabrics should be tested for water and light fastness.

**Table 7-5 Fabric**

| Fabric | Recommended | Not Recommended |
|---|---|---|
| Undyed cotton | x | |
| Linen | x | |
| Polyester | x | |
| Cotton-polyester | x | |
| Wool | | x |
| Silk | | x |
| Fire retardant treatments | | x |
| Permanent press and shrink proof fabrics | | x |
| Treated fabrics | | x |

Recommended:

a. *Undyed cotton*

b. *Linen*

c. *Polyester*

d. *Cotton-polyester*

Not Recommended:

a. *Wool*—emits sulphur compounds and tarnishes silver.

b. *Silk*—acidic and may have pesticides.

c. *Fire retardant treatments*—may contain disodium phosphate.

d. *Permanent press and shrink proof fabrics*—may contain urea formaldehyde.

e. *Treated Fabrics*

Treated fabrics, such as those treated against mildew and moths may emit formic acid and/or acetic acid.

## 7.5.2 Seal

**Recommended:** Silicone sealant is recommended for sealing exhibit cases. Conditioned silica gel can be used to stabilize the relative humidity in cases. Indicating gel is especially useful for showing when the gel has reached the saturation point.

## 7.5.3 Gaskets

Recommended:

a. *Acrylic*

b. *Teflon*

c. *Silicone*

d. *Neoprene*

Not Recommended:

e. *Rubber*

## 7.5.4 Felt

**Recommended:** Synthetic felt for construction and mounting.

**Not Recommended:** Wool felt.

## 7.5.5 Foam

**Recommended:** Polyethylene cross-linked with radiation or foamed with inert gas or another approved inert foam.

## 7.5.6 Adhesives

**Recommended:** Acrylics or hot-melt glues.

**Not Recommended:** Protein glues or cellulose nitrate.

## 7.6 LABORATORY(S)

Laboratories will be occupied by staff and temporarily by archival collections. Floor materials and finishes should be durable, attractive, and easy to clean and maintain. As much as possible, care should be taken to develop an environment that is identical to the stacks. The prohibited materials and finishes listed in Appendix A should be avoided in areas where records are used and treated.

## 7.6.1 Floors

**Recommended:**

a. *Concrete*

Sealed and epoxy covered concrete as described for use in stacks in Section 7.3.1 is also desirable flooring for laboratories for its safe, inert, and durable qualities. However, there may be instances that certain laboratory equipment requires a different kind of flooring. Also, in older buildings the structure may dictate that some other kind of floor covering be used in these spaces.

b. *Tiles*

Ceramic tiles are often used in wet areas of laboratories. Care should be taken in specifying the adhesive and grout used for ceramic tiles in labs. Select those where the total volatile organic compounds off-gassed from the tiles and adhesives does not exceed 100 micrograms per square meter.

**Not Recommended:**

c. *Carpet:* See Section 7.3.1.

d. *Wood:* See Section 7.3.1.

## 7.6.2 Walls, Ceilings, and Exposed Pipes

**Recommended:**

a. *Latex-based paints*

Latex-based paints are recommended for the walls, ceilings, and exposed pipes in laboratories. If concrete block walls are used in the laboratories, they should be primed and painted with latex-based paint to prevent dust. Ceiling pipes should be coated with an acrylic primer (water reducible) and covered with latex paint.

b. *Ceramic tile*

Ceramic tile walls should use an adhesive and grout that emits low VOCs as noted in Section 7.6.1.

**Not Recommended:**

c. *Oil-based or alkyd paints:* See Section 7.3.2.

## 7.6.3 Furniture

**Recommended:**

a. *Steel*

Stainless steel or metal furniture and shelving, finished with an electrostatically applied powder coating, is recommended for use in laboratories.

b. *Anodized aluminum*

Uncoated anodized aluminum is extremely strong, yet light in weight. The metal is believed to be nonreactive and without a coating so there are no off-gassing problems

**Not Recommended:**

c. *Wood*

Solid wood and composite wood products are not recommended for use in laboratories for the same reasons discussed for stacks. Follow the guidelines outlined in Section 7.3.1.

d. *Fabrics*

Upholstered chairs and use of fabrics should be avoided in laboratories for the same reasons discussed for stacks and exhibits. Follow the guidelines outlined in Sections 7.3.5 and 7.5.1.

## 7.6.4 Countertops

There are a number of options for laboratory countertops depending on the type of work being done. Generally, laboratory countertops should be made of a material that is nonporous and heat and scratch resistant. The countertops should be sealed on all sides, including the bottom, and contain no adhesive residues. The countertops should have rounded corners and there should not be any protrusions.

**Recommended:**

a. *Epoxy resin*

The most commonly used countertop is epoxy resin, which usually comes in black, but can also be obtained in gray and white.

b. *Solid surfaces*

Solid surfaces such as Dupont's Corian countertops are appropriate for applications such as conservation work; it is offered in a number of colors.

c. *Stainless steel*

Stainless steel is a more expensive option, but is very useful for certain applications in lab work. The edges should be rolled.

**Acceptable:**

d. *Plastic-laminated panels*—such as plywood with phenoic laminates (e.g., Formica).

**Not Acceptable:**

e. *Natural stones*—such as granite and marble.

The natural stones and marbles are porous so must be sealed. In addition, they are cold to the touch and are susceptible to chipping and dust.

## 7.7 READING ROOM(S)

Reading rooms will be occupied by staff and visitors while they temporarily review archival collections. Floor materials and finishes should be durable, attractive, and easy to clean. As much as possible, care should be taken to develop an environment that is similar to the stacks, understanding that the area also needs warmth, inviting décor, and sound absorption. The prohibited materials and finishes listed in Appendix A should be avoided in areas where records are temporarily reviewed. However, in general, because the collection materials are out for short periods of time, the guidelines for reading rooms are not as stringent as other areas of the archival facility.

### 7.7.1 Floors

**Acceptable:**

a. *Carpet*

Low pile carpet or carpet tiles are recommended if carpet is used in reading rooms. Book trucks and carts should be able to easily travel across the floor. Low or no VOC products that meet the Carpet and Rug Institute's Indoor Air Quality Standards (Green Label Program) should be specified. The carpet adhesive should be non-wet adhesive, micro-encapsulated tackifier impregnated into cushion backing solvent-free adhesive (as recommended by manufacturer) for interior installation of vinyl backed carpet. Acrylic-based adhesive must be nonflammable, water-based, and alkali-resistant, mildew-resistant, freeze-thaw stable. Adhesive should release from substrate without leaving residue.

b. *Wood*

Wood floors should be limited to the fullest possible extent in reading rooms to prevent damage to the holdings. Any sealant or finish applied to wood flooring should attempt to limit the off-gassing of formaldehyde to no more than 48.8 parts per billion [61.0 micrograms per cubic meter] and limit the total volatile organic compounds off-gassed to not exceed 500 micrograms per square meter.

### 7.7.2 Walls and Ceilings

**Recommended:** Latex-based paints.

**Not Recommended:** Oil-based or alkyd paints.

### 7.7.3 Furniture

Solid wood and composite wood products are not recommended for use in reading rooms for the same reasons as noted for stacks. In general, when possible, follow the guidelines outlined in Section 7.3.1. However, wood is often used for furniture because it is readily available, easy to work with, and attractive.

If the budget allows, select wood that is comparatively low in harmful emissions. Certain softwoods, such as poplar and basswood, are recommended. Only one hardwood, African mahogany, is low in volatiles. Oak is the most acidic wood and potentially the most dangerous. (The Canadian Conservation Institute has a chart that lists the acidity of different wood species.) Additional measures should be taken to limit the off-gassing and acidity if wood products are present. Choose a sealant that does not give off problematic volatiles of its own. In general, avoid oil-based products, including sealants, paints, and stains. Coatings generally considered safe are moisture-borne polyurethanes and two-part epoxy sealants. Not all polyurethanes are safe, however, and new products should be tested for chemical stability. Select those for which the off-gassing of formaldehyde is no more than 48.8 parts per billion [61 micrograms per cubic meter]. Select those where the total volatile organic compounds off-gassed from the tiles and adhesives does not exceed 500 micrograms per square meter.

Plywood and other wood composites are even more problematic than solid wood because they may be fabricated with adhesives or resins containing formaldehyde, which oxidizes to formic acid. If plywood is used, follow the guidelines in Section 7.4.3. Additional measures should be taken to limit the off-gassing and acidity if wood products are present. Choose a sealant that does not give off problematic volatiles of its own. In general, avoid oil-based products, including sealants, paints, and stains. Coatings generally considered safe are moisture-borne polyurethanes and two-part epoxy sealants. Not all polyurethanes are safe, however, and new products should be tested for chemical stability. Select those that the off-gassing of formaldehyde is no more than 48.8 parts per billion or 61 micrograms per cubic meter. Select those where the total VOCs off-gassed from the tiles and adhesives does not exceed 500 micrograms per square meter.

If wood shelving is selected for reading rooms, it should only be used to house non-unique materials and should be treated with the appropriate sealant.

## 7.8 MITIGATION STRATEGIES

Achieving optimum conditions in an archives facility can be difficult and expensive. It is important to remember that even small steps taken to improve conditions in a facility will benefit the entire collection. As much as possible, select and use materials and finishes that have low levels of VOC emissions. If areas are at risk in the facility, the following measures will help:

- Increase the number of air changes per hour.

- Reduce the relative humidity, but do not go lower than 30% RH (see Section 3).

- Use absorption materials, such as activated carbon or sodium bicarbonate (baking soda).

- Install gas-phased filters in the heating and air-conditioning system.

Section 8

# STORAGE EQUIPMENT

*Michele F. Pacifico*

## 8.1 RATIONALE

A majority of the space within archival facilities is dedicated to the safe storage of archival collections. A major challenge for archivists is to store and protect the collections while still making the records accessible to researchers. A key component in this strategy is the records storage equipment that includes shelving, cases, cabinets, racks, and other furniture that support the collections.

Storage equipment is a long-term investment that provides safe storage and an efficient layout for archival collections. Careful planning is crucial in selecting appropriate products. Shelving and accompanying storage furniture should be planned to meet the specific needs of the archival facility and reflect the size and quantity of its collections.

## 8.2 SHELVING SYSTEMS

Archival shelving can be either static or mobile with the latter having either a manual or an electrically operated carriage system. The choice of a shelving system depends on a number of factors, including space, budget, and technical considerations. Static or fixed shelving is less expensive to purchase and install but requires a larger floor area than mobile shelving. Mobile or compact shelving, on the other hand, can store more records in a smaller space thereby saving on initial construction cost and the long-term costs for heating, air conditioning, and facility maintenance. Mobile shelving may increase records retrieval time but it can provide greater security to specific sections of storage. Mobile shelving requires a heavier floor load than static shelving and may not be feasible in existing buildings. Refer to Section 2.4.5 for guidelines to floor loads for stacks. Both systems are appropriate for archival facilities.

## 8.3 MATERIALS AND FINISHES

Steel is the most commonly used shelving material in archival facilities. It should be finished with an electrostatically applied powder coated finish to avoid the off-gassing problems associated with baked enamel. Other options for shelving and cabinets in the archival environment are chrome-plated steel and anodized aluminum shelving. Refer to Sections 7.3.5 and 7.3.6 for guidelines to the materials and finishes for the shelving, cabinets, and carts used in stacks.

## 8.4 CONSTRUCTION AND PERFORMANCE

Whether static or mobile, archival shelving units should have similar construction and performance requirements. Archival shelving and furniture should have smooth, nonabrasive finishes that are resistant to chipping. Equipment should be free of sharp exposed edges and protrusions such as exposed nuts and bolts that are hazardous to staff and the records.

Archival shelving must be designed to withstand the design weight of the records without failure and should be braced and secured to prevent deflection, lean, or collapse when all shelves are full. Shelving supports should be strong enough to not bend or warp when units are full. Specifications for the design and testing of shelving are based on American National Standards Institute (ANSI) MH 28.2 (*Specification for the Design and Testing of Metal-Wood Shelving*, 2003). In addition, shelving must be laterally braced to protect against seismic forces as outlined by the pertinent building codes.

### 8.4.1 Shelving Bays

Typical shelving units are made up of shelves and uprights with cross braces at the rear and ends of the shelving. Shelving units should have kick panels at the bottom of each bay or unit. Each range may have metal end panels.

Optimal space utilization uses double faced (back-to-back) rows eliminating an aisle. Such units should be bolted or clipped together through adjoining uprights. Cross bracing and metal dividers should not be used between double faced bays where it allows pass through storage between bays for oversized materials.

The construction criteria for shelving are

- uprights and bracing: minimum 16-gauge steel;

- shelf thickness: 18 to 22 gauge depending on the requirements of the stacks;

- shelves: should have a maximum structural deflection of L/320 (length of shelf divided by 320). All shelves should be fully adjustable in one inch increments with a maximum of adjustability of one and a half inch intervals. For paper-based materials, a 16-by-40-inch [41-by-102-centimeter] shelf should have a minimum load bearing capacity of 200 pounds [91 kilograms] per shelf.

### 8.4.2 Mobile Shelving Rails

Mobile shelving moves on wheeled carriages over low-profile steel rails. In new construction, they should be recessed in concrete floors. In existing or remodeled facilities, the rails are installed over the existing floor requiring the installation of platforms that are built up to track levels. The platforms allow the carts to be easily wheeled over the rails and prevent people from tripping over the rails.

Platforms made of steel or aluminum are preferred. Platforms made of plywood are not recommended for stacks. Refer to Section 7.3. Regardless of installation method, it is critical that the rails be level to prevent drift or movement of the carriages.

### 8.4.3 Mobile Shelving Carriages

The carriages of the mobile shelving system must be constructed with a sufficient strength-to-weight ratio to prevent binding, racking, and misalignment. Shelving carriages should have a maximum structural deflection of L/320. There should be no fasteners that can loosen or break. The system must carry the specified weight of the collections stored on it without distortion and should evenly transfer the weight onto the wheels. The wheels must be balanced for a smooth operation of the carriages.

## 8.5 LAYOUT

Shelving comes in a variety of sizes. A shelving plan should be developed to identify the various sizes and quantities of shelving needed in an archival facility and to provide an efficient shelving layout for the stacks. Before the final layout, designers must check the Occupational Safety and Health Administration (OSHA), state, and local regulations to ensure compliance.

### 8.5.1 Configuration

The shelving should be arranged in configurations that make maximum use of the floor space while still conforming to fire and life safety regulations. Shelving is usually arranged in rectangular blocks with one or more main transportation aisles. Shelving bays should be placed at least 1 inch from any wall in a stack area to avoid heat and cold radiation and to protect collections from water running down the walls from overhead leaks. If the outer stack wall is an exterior wall, it is recommended that a distance of 18 inches [46 centimeters] be maintained between the shelving and the exterior wall.

Shelving ranges should never be

- located under water pipes (unless drip pans are provided and tied into the building drain system);
- located against uninsulated outside walls;
- located against heat sources.

## 8.5.2 Width of Main Aisles

The widths of the main aisles in stacks are different depending on the type of shelving system used:

- Static or mobile shelving—main aisles should be at least 48 inches [1.2 meters] wide.

- High bay mobile shelving—main aisles should be at least 12 feet [3.7 meters] wide to allow space for retrieval equipment.

## 8.5.3 Width of Stack Aisles

The widths of the aisles between ranges of shelving in stacks are different depending on the type of shelving system and/or the size of the records being stored:

- Stack aisles should be a minimum of 36 inches [91 centimeters] wide.

- For the storage of oversized records the stack aisles may need to be wider to safely access the records.

- For high shelves that require the use of lifts to access the records, the stack aisle should be a minimum of 52 inches [1.3 meters] to accommodate the lift and its operation.

## 8.5.4 Length of Stack Aisles

The maximum length of the stack aisles for any archival facility will be dictated by the footprint of the facility, the location of entrances and exits, codes for egress and life safety, the type of shelving system, and the program requirements of the staff for accessibility. The longer the stack aisles, the more time it takes staff to retrieve records. However, long aisles provide great records storage density within a stack. Under the current U.S. life safety codes the length of a stack aisle can be no longer than 200 feet [61 meters]. (Note: Under the current International Building Codes [IBC] the length of a stack aisle is set at no more than 20 feet [6.1 meters]. However, this is based on office criteria and the United States is trying to change this code.)

Mobile storage systems that are manually operated are limited to ranges measuring up to 45 feet [13.7 meters] in length. Longer ranges can be used in electrically operated systems and can be as long as desired by the user within code restrictions.

## 8.6 DIMENSIONS

### 8.6.1 Height of Shelving Bays

Ideally, the height of the shelving in an archival facility should be set so that the average person can reach the top shelf without the aid of a footstool or ladder. The standard shelving height in archives has traditionally been 84 to 90 inches [2.1 to 2.3 meters] high providing 7 shelves that are 12 inches [30 centimeters] apart.

However, archival shelving is often installed with taller shelving and increased density because of the increasing costs for land, construction, operations, and maintenance. The height of the shelving in archival facilities is often determined by the building's footprint. With high ceilings, archives planners may opt to install shelving that is higher than 90 inches [2.3 meters] thereby providing more storage space per square foot for records. Each addition of another shelf above 7 feet [2.1 meters] increases the total storage capacity of a stack by more than 14 percent.

Some archival facilities have successfully used static high bay systems with shelving heights over 40 feet [12.2 meters] high (e.g., stacks at Utah State Archives are 45 feet [13.7 meters] in height). Static high bay systems require mezzanines, lifts, or a mechanical retrieval system.

The newest option for archival storage is high bay electric mobile shelving systems. Recent fire tests show that high bay electric mobile shelving can safely go 30 feet [9.1 meters] high providing 30 shelves per bay of shelving without the addition of in-rack sprinkler installations as long as the archival materials are stored in boxes. Refer to Section 4.8.2.2 for guidelines for fire protection for mobile high bay shelving.

Additional height to the shelving units has an impact on collection accessibility. Stools, ladders, or lifts will be needed to allow staff to reach the higher shelves.

## 8.6.2 Height of Bottom Shelf above the Floor

The lowest shelf in a shelving bay should be at least 3 inches [8 centimeters] above the floor to prevent damage to the collections from flooding.

## 8.6.3 Vertical Storage Space between the Shelves

Shelves are usually spaced 12 inches [30.5 centimeters] apart for textual records. It is recommended that a minimum of 11 inches [28 centimeters] of clear vertical storage space be provided between each level of installed shelves. All shelves should be adjustable so that adjustments can be made for nonstandard sized boxes, volumes, and special media records.

## 8.6.4 Shelf Size

Archives should maximize their storage capacity with a standard sized shelf that accommodates the use of archival boxes, records center type boxes, and some special media records. Specialized shelving sizes may be required for oversized and special media records.

For records stored in standard sized archives boxes or records center boxes, the most common shelf size measures 16 inches deep by 40 inches [41 by 102 centimeters] wide. However, there are other effective shelf size options that can be considered depending on stack size and configuration, access requirements, frequency of use, size of the collections and the budget. Shelving boxes double deep and double high requires a different shelving sizes.

- Shelf depth: A 16-inch [41-centimeter] shelf depth insures that standard archival boxes will not extend beyond the face of the shelf. When installed as double faced units without cross bracing or dividers, the width of the two, back-to-back shelves is 32 inches [81 centimeters]. In high bay mobile shelving a stop is needed on the back of the 16-inch [41-centimeter] shelf because of the 6-inch [15-centimeter] gap needed between the two shelving units for fire safety. For many manufacturers, their standard shelf product measures 15 inches [38 centimeters] deep. On fixed shelving, archives boxes will overhang a 15-inch [38-centimeter] shelf risking box damage. On mobile shelving, there is the additional risk of equipment malfunction as box overhang on a 15-inch [38-centimeter] shelf will not allow carriages to fully close.

- Shelf length: The 40-inch [102-centimeter] shelf should provide at least 38 inches [97 centimeters] of clear horizontal storage space. A 40-inch [102-centimeter] shelf will house 3 records center boxes or 7 archives boxes. For many manufacturers, their standard shelving lengths are a 36-inch [91-centimeter] library shelf and a 42-inch [107-centimeter] shelf for archives. A 42-inch [107-centimeter] shelf will hold 3 records center boxes or 8 archives boxes. With a 42-inch [107-centimeter] shelf there is some loss of efficiency if storing record center boxes.

## 8.7 ACCESSORIES

The basic shelving system can come with a number of accessories that help maintain the records on the shelves or help staff when referencing records. Available accessories include

- book supports to aid in keeping volumes upright on the shelf;
- pull out (or sliding) work shelves to aid staff that need to review documents within the shelving aisle;
- video cassette shelves to aid in efficient storage of videos.

## 8.8 OVERSIZED RECORDS

Oversized records require the use of specially-sized shelving or cabinets. The recommendations for the construction, performance, safety, and use of oversized shelving are the same as those for more standard sized archival shelving. The guidelines in Sections 8.2 through 8.6 apply to the storage of oversized records. Refer to Sections 7.3.5 and 7.3.6 for guidelines on shelving and cabinet materials and finishes.

### 8.8.1 Flat Files/Map Cases

Maps, plans, and oversized drawings should be stored, wherever possible, unrolled and unfolded. Optimum storage for these types of documents is in shallow drawers in flat files or map cabinets. Flat files can be fixed and stacked or installed on mobile carriages.

- Aisle width between rows of flat files must be wide enough to accommodate a fully opened drawer and room for a person to safely retrieve an oversized record from the drawer.

- Drawers in flat files should be no more than two inches deep, and less if possible. The deeper the drawer the greater the weight on the items and the more difficult it is to remove an oversized document from the drawer.

- Drawers should have stops to prevent them from coming out of the cabinets.

- Drawers should open and close smoothly, preventing vibration to items.

- Drawers should have dust covers or rear hood to prevent items from being damaged at the back of the drawer.

### 8.8.2 Racking Systems

When oversized records and framed items are stored vertically on racking systems, provisions must be made to support the weight of the document on all sides.

## 8.9 COLD STORAGE SHELVING

Open, through-style chrome-plated stainless-steel wire racks are recommended for boxed material housed in cold storage areas, usually those with temperatures below 50°F [10°C]. The chrome shelving provides good air circulation and prevents condensation from settling on the containers. The recommendations for the construction, performance, safety, and use of chrome-plated shelving are the same as those for more standard-sized archival shelving.

## 8.10 CABINETS

The recommendations for construction, performance, safety, and use of special cabinets are the same as those for more standard sized archival shelving.

Section 9

# FUNCTIONAL SPACES

*David Carmicheal*

9.1 **RATIONALE**

Archival facilities must balance collections preservation with the needs of researcher access and use. This balance begins from the time the records arrive on the loading dock to inspection and storage; it continues as staff arranges and describes the records, prepares finding aids, and performs conservation treatments; and it reaches a critical point when the public gains access to the records through research or public display.

The movement of records into and through the facility involves many different functional spaces. Some, like loading docks and processing rooms, address the records directly; others, such as lunchrooms and restrooms, support the work of visitors and staff.

In most archival facilities, greater attention is paid to records storage and public spaces, where the collections are obviously vulnerable to theft, damage, and other hazards. Less attention is paid to spaces where records reside outside of secure storage but are not exposed to public access. Archivists and designers should pay close attention to these spaces and consider whether original records will be permitted into these areas and under what conditions. Laboratories, obviously, must accommodate original records, and must be designed to ensure proper access and environmental controls. But archivists must decide whether records will be permitted in areas such as training rooms or staff offices, and if so, these spaces must be designed to protect the records. A clear policy, supplemented by clear signage, will enhance the safety of original records.

## 9.2 LOADING DOCK

The loading dock's primary mission is to provide a secure environment for receiving archival collections into the building and to act as a barrier against weather conditions; it may secondarily serve as a transition space for incoming supplies and equipment, outgoing records, and related activities. Archival records moving through the loading dock must be protected from theft or unauthorized access, inclement weather, pests, and accidental disposal.

### 9.2.1 Design Criteria

Loading docks get a lot of use in an archival facility. Special care should be taken to design them so that the records are adequately protected. The loading dock should be designed with

- a covered concrete platform with one or more bays for servicing various sizes of trucks;

- covers or canopies over the loading dock platform that extend at least 4 feet [1.2 meters] beyond the edge of the platform; should be a minimum of 14 feet [4.3 meters] clear (not including space for overhead lighting, ductwork, etc.);

- a covered platform that is placed on the exterior of the building. The covered platform will prevent fumes and fuel from entering the archives building and will protect records from inclement weather during offloading;

- a ramp leading to the dock that is sloped away from the building and drained sufficiently to prevent storm water from collecting near, or migrating into, the building;

- positive air pressure;

- separate air handling system, vented directly to the outside, so that debris and pollutants cannot affect archival areas;

- a conditioned exterior, especially against high heat and humidity, if the records are to be left on the loading dock for more than one day.

Care must be taken so that both the exterior and interior platforms of the loading dock are isolated from the rest of the archival facility to prevent unauthorized entry, pest and rodent migration, and unconditioned and polluted air from reaching archival areas. Refer to Section 2.6.7 for details on mechanical systems.

Ideally, the archives facility should provide separate loading docks for handling archival holdings and for the transport of food and trash collection. If this is not possible, and the dock serves both functions, careful thought should be given to how the archival records will be protected from accidental damage or disposal. Designated areas to temporarily place only archival records or only non-archival materials should be indicated by highly visible floor coloring, fences, or other boundary markers. If the loading dock is used to receive food, provide designated pathways to prevent food from passing through records holding areas or exhibit spaces.

## 9.2.2 Size

The loading dock must be of adequate size to receive the largest anticipated transfer of records. Unless a separate receiving room is provided (Section 9.3), the dock should be large enough for records to be inspected and verified against transmittal lists.

## 9.2.3 Location/Adjacencies

The loading dock should be

- located near the stacks;
- located on the same level as the stacks and/or close to freight or large elevators that service stacks;
- adjacent to any inspection and isolation spaces;
- located so that noise does not migrate into public and staff work spaces.

In addition, it is useful to have toilet facilities at or near the loading dock so that drivers and others need not enter the main part of the building.

### 9.2.4 Doors

All loading dock doors, roll-up and swing, should have appropriate security and be installed with weather stripping. In addition, the doors should have brush sweeps to keep out insects, vermin, and molds. Polypropylene bird netting should be used around exterior roll doors and loading dock areas to prevent birds and bats from entering the building.

If the loading dock is adjacent to sensitive spaces, such as laboratories or stacks, interlocking roll-up doors (in which one door can be raised only if the other is lowered) should be installed at opposite ends of the dock to prevent unconditioned outside air from reaching conditioned spaces. Interior doors should be a minimum of 36 inches [91 centimeters] wide. In addition, there should be at least one door leading from the dock into the facility that is a double door with a minimum 6-foot- [1.8-meters-] wide opening.

## 9.3 RECEIVING

If space allows, a receiving or staging room adjacent to the loading dock should be designated for receiving records; inspecting incoming records for security risks, pests, mold, and damage; verifying transmittal forms; and unpacking records.

### 9.3.1 Design Criteria

The receiving room should be designed with

- washable floors and walls;

- floor drain;

- fire and smoke protection similar to stack areas. Refer to Section 4;

- separate air handling system from archival areas;

- insulation to prevent migration of pests and mold;

- doors with weather stripping.

The receiving room should be large enough to house

- shelving;
- large movable tables;
- clearly marked trash cans (to distinguish them from records boxes);
- computer station.

## 9.3.2 Isolation

Within the receiving area, ideally a separate room, there should be a space designated for isolating contaminated records. The isolation room should have the same design criteria as the receiving room and should contain a biological safety cabinet in which materials with mold can be stored and cleaned.

## 9.4 SUPPLY STORAGE

Adequate space should be provided for the storage of non-records equipment and supplies. Experience shows that the amount of space required for the storage of non-record equipment and supplies and is often grossly underestimated during design. Storage can take a form other than closets. Office supplies can be stored in centralized copy/fax areas if proper cabinets are included. Processing supplies can be stored in cabinets or on shelves in processing areas or in a warehouse area. Some laboratory supplies may need specially vented cabinets. Equipment and added stock can be stored in a warehouse area, often located near the loading dock. Some storage spaces (such as those for office supplies) may be accessible to staff, while others (like computer storage) may be restricted.

The following materials need to be stored:

- Archival supplies such as document cases, folders, and acid-free papers.
- Office supplies, equipment not yet installed (spare computers and printers, etc.), and extra chairs and tables.

- Staff party supplies and decorations (a proper storage place will discourage the storage of these items in stacks).

- Laboratory supplies, including chemicals.

- Attic stock, such as extra tile, floor covering, Heating, Ventilation, and Air-Conditioning filters, etc.

- Paint, fuel, and lawn care equipment—provide secure storage exterior to the building.

## 9.5 SERVICE CORRIDORS

Corridors leading from the loading dock to the stacks, and any corridor through which records will be moved, must be of adequate width to accommodate pallet jacks and other records moving equipment. Service corridors should be at least 8 feet [2.4 meters] wide, although 10 feet [3 meters] is recommended for primary corridors and 8 feet [2.4 meters] for secondary corridors. Corridors should be a minimum of 10 feet [3 meters] high.

Corridor floors must be level and constructed of durable materials that can withstand the heavy traffic of pallet jacks and other records moving equipment. Corridor walls should be sealed concrete or constructed of materials capable of withstanding collisions with book trucks and carts.

## 9.6 ELEVATORS

Multistory archival facilities should have at least one freight elevator and may require additional elevators for staff and visitors.

### 9.6.1 Freight Elevator(s)

The freight elevator(s) should be located adjacent to the loading dock with easy access to stacks. Consideration should also be given to the location of exhibit galleries and other support areas. Freight elevators must be designed with adequate capacity to transport the largest anticipated load of records between floors.

Section 9—Functional Spaces 139

## 9.6.2 Passenger Elevator(s)

Multistory archival facilities must also have additional and sufficient elevators for all public areas, and for staff work areas that do not directly involve the transporting of archival materials. Depending on the size and design of the building, another elevator(s) may be necessary for transporting records to and from reading rooms, processing rooms, and laboratories.

## 9.7 LABORATORY(S)

Larger archival facilities often include laboratories for conservation and preservation work on paper-based and special media records. Smaller facilities may include a space for restoration work. Designers should provide appropriate space, whether it will be used for complex treatments or to produce simple enclosures. Design of a conservation laboratory is complex and individualized and any design must be in consultation with a conservator.

### 9.7.1 Design Criteria

Laboratories in archival facilities should be designed with

- separate air handling systems;
- floor loads that can accommodate heavy laboratory equipment;
- waterproof and skid-resistant floors;
- floor drains with catch drains and grilles in case of flooding;
- chemical storage cabinets (may need special ventilation);
- separate spaces for wet and dry work;
- at least one 6-foot- [1.8-meter-] wide door to allow for collections and supply movement into and out of the laboratory;
- filtered and/or deionized water;
- under-sink water heater to provide 150°F [65°C] water;
- eyewash(es);

- 220-volt power for special equipment;

- adequate storage space for large and bulky conservation materials; storage may take up as much as one-third to one-half the size of the lab itself;

- shelving for reference books;

- one or more administrative offices or spaces immediately adjacent to the lab itself so that the staff can keep administrative work separate from laboratory work.

Conservation labs may request natural sunlight for some treatment work; windows must be carefully planned and must be ultraviolet filtered and outfitted with shades or blinds. Refer to Section 6.3 for laboratory lighting guidelines. In addition, an archival lab may need a shower and drain for emergency use and the use of ceiling-mounted outlets on flexible cables. Treatment work is very interesting to the visiting public and some archival facilities provide interior windows from the corridor into the laboratory for public observation.

## 9.7.2 Size

The size of the laboratory will depend on the size of the holdings and the kind of work done by the institution. In general, laboratory space should be as open as possible and unencumbered by posts and pillars. Generous circulation space will be needed for moving large objects, such as maps and special treatment carts.

## 9.7.3 Location/Adjacencies

Laboratories must not be located above stacks, processing rooms, or exhibit areas. Labs use water and chemicals and should be designed to prevent leaks.

## 9.7.4 Furniture

Care must be taken with the kind of furniture put into archival laboratories. Refer to Section 7 for information on materials and finishes. In general, avoid fixed furniture except along the walls. Cabinets should have under counter lighting. Tables should be movable, adjustable-height and have heavy-duty locking wheels. Vented, locked cabinets must be provided for chemical storage. Two cabinets should be provided to separately store incompatible materials.

### 9.7.5 Equipment

The laboratory may contain some or all of the following equipment (this list is not comprehensive):

- Fume hood with hooded venting system
- Elephant trunks (flexible snorkels for capturing light particles and vapors)
- Humidification chamber
- Drying racks
- Workbenches
- Movable tables
- Book press
- Chemical-resistant sinks
- Carts and cart storage
- Wall and mobile units for rolled conservation supplies
- Photographic documentation equipment
- Microscope
- Paper cutter
- Ultrasonic welder
- Suction table
- Guillotine
- Drill press
- Leaf caster
- Board shears

- Mat cutters
- Box making machine
- Mobile task lighting
- Environmental monitoring equipment
- Storage for supplies, tools, and chemicals.

## 9.8 REFORMATTING LAB

Spaces for scanning and microfilming archival records must be convenient to the stacks and should be designed to protect the original records. Reformatting areas generally require

- shelving for the short-term storage of collections being reformatted;
- furniture for preparing the documents for reformatting;
- space for a variety of scanning equipment to accommodate all sizes of documents and format types, including microfilm, slides, prints, negatives, and books;
- space for handling large groups of documents or individual oversized documents;
- data connections and electrical outlets of a rating compatible with the planned reformatting equipment;
- dimmable lighting.

## 9.9 PROCESSING ROOM(S)

Processing rooms provide separate work space from stacks and office areas where staff may work individually or in groups to examine, sort, arrange, describe, and rehouse archival materials. Since archival materials may be stored in processing rooms for extended periods of time, careful attention should be paid to the environmental conditions, security, and finishes in these spaces. These should match or closely approximate conditions in the stacks, although the temperature set for stacks may be too low for human comfort in processing rooms. Refer to Sections 3, 5, 7, and 8.

Processing rooms should include

- large, movable tables for sorting records;
- shelving to hold records, boxes, and archival supplies;
- adequate open space for parking book trucks and other carts;
- space to accommodate the maximum number of staff who may work on one collection at one time.

In addition, processing rooms might include

- counter or table space for computers, and computer connections;
- any equipment required for processing special-format materials, such as audiovisual materials.

The processing room should include, or be convenient to, copying facilities.

## 9.10  COMPUTER ROOM

The computer room houses network file servers, routers, and other equipment supporting the computer network. It must have an uninterruptible power supply and be connected to computers in the rest of the building via a Main Distribution Frame and, if building size requires, one or more Intermediate Distribution Frames. The computer room should be designed with

- raised access flooring with anti-static floor covering, if conditions permit;
- power outlets with flexible tails;
- computer-grade circuits;
- a plan for wireless networks to be incorporated to provide maximum flexibility;
- temperature no greater than 70°F [21°C];
- no windows.

## 9.11 STAFF SPACES

Staff spaces should be comparable in size and quality to standard office building space. In certain situations (government construction, in particular) office sizes are determined by written policy. All staff spaces should be strictly separated from public spaces and should be off limits to the public without proper escort.

### 9.11.1 Staff Locker Room

Some archives require staff to place personal items in lockers. In such cases, the staff locker room should be located near the staff entrance and secured from other portions of the building. Even if staff is not required to use lockers, consider providing locker rooms and showers for staff use, to encourage exercise, walking, and biking to work.

### 9.11.2 Staff Restrooms/Quiet Spaces

Staff restrooms, like public restrooms (Section 9.13.3), should never be located over or near stacks and records use areas, though they should be in reasonable proximity to staff work spaces. Consider providing a separate Quiet Room where staff may tend to medical or special needs; equip the room with electrical outlets, a lockable door, a lounger, and a sink.

### 9.11.3 Staff Lunchroom

Even in archival facilities with cafeterias, staff lunchrooms are often provided so that the staff does not store food at their workstations and has a private place to eat away from their workstations. Sometimes the space doubles as a staff meeting room.

The lunchroom should be separate from stacks or other spaces where records are used. Because of fire hazards such as microwaves and coffeepots, appropriate fire detection and suppression are needed. The lunchroom should be maintained at slightly negative pressure and, if possible, should be vented directly to the outside of the building. If possible, locate the lunchroom near outside windows.

The staff lunchroom should include

- sink, refrigerator, microwave, and coffee pot;
- tables and chairs;
- recycle center;
- space for posting safety notices, personnel rules, and other items of interest to the entire staff.

### 9.11.4 Staff Library

Consider providing a room with shelving for books and journals for staff use. Include at least one table and several chairs. The staff library can double as a group project space or a meeting room.

### 9.11.5 Staff Offices

Environmental and lighting conditions outlined elsewhere in this guideline extend to staff offices. The most important consideration is whether original records will be allowed in these spaces and under what conditions? Once that policy decision is made, the proper conditions can be planned for these spaces.

### 9.11.6 Shared Work Spaces

Shared work spaces include staff meeting and conference rooms, project rooms, and fax/copy/mail areas. Project rooms can double as processing areas and meeting spaces if they are designed to meet the environmental and security conditions of processing areas. Provide shelving for records and at least one large table that can be used for conferencing or for arranging records. Centralized copy/fax/mail areas can include counter space and cabinets for storage of supplies or mail distribution.

## 9.12 READING ROOM(S)

Reading rooms are secure spaces that are used by the public to review archival materials. They are designed so that the records are protected at all times. Each archival facility will have its own unique requirements depending on its collection, the space available for research activities, and its security and researcher policies. While many archives will provide a single room for researchers to consult a variety of archival formats, larger archives may provide separate spaces for specific media type of record. Some archives will function with one reading room for textual holdings and a second for non-textual holdings. Others will have separate rooms for each format—textual, microfilm, audiovisual, and oversized records—as well as spaces for holding and copying records.

Reading rooms and their support spaces should be

- accessible from the public entrance and/or lobby of the archival facility. The public should not be permitted to walk through or by secure stacks and other records holding areas;

- accessible through a single entrance;

- located close to staff offices, and when possible, designed to make the transport of records to the rooms secure and easy for staff;

- located in a quiet area of the facility and designed with soundproofing.

Each repository will have policies outlining the use of the collections and some of them will be directly related to the layout and function of the reading room spaces. Refer to Section 5 for specific security requirements for reading rooms; Section 6 for lighting requirements; and Section 7 regarding the materials and finishes for reading rooms.

## 9.12.1 Researcher Registration/Orientation and Consultation

Space is needed for researchers to provide registration information, be briefed on the archives' rules and regulations for research, and to consult with staff on individual research requirements. Some repositories show a film as part of their orientation process. Design criteria for this space include

- adjacent to textual reading room and other reading rooms;

- adjacent to finding aids or co-located with finding aids;

- sound insulation to prevent disrupting other researchers;

- windows into research areas to allow staff to visually monitor reading rooms;
- data access through cabling or wireless connections.

Some archival facilities split these operations and locate researcher registration and orientation adjacent to the lobby and locate consultation activities near the reading rooms and finding aids. Refer to Section 9.12.4.

## 9.12.2 Textual Reading Room

Researchers consult paper-based archival records in a textual reading room. The records can be a variety of sizes and formats—loose papers in archival boxes, books, large fragile volumes, periodicals, etc. In general a textual reading room should have

- few visual barriers to provide a clear field of view for staff to observe researchers in all parts of the room;
- automatic door openers for the service doors into the room. If oversized materials are researched in the textual reading room, provide double doors;
- staff operated reference desk located centrally within the room so that staff have a clear line of sight to all areas of the room. The reference desk may have a silent alarm button that links it to building security. It should have room for a computer, supplies, and any other operational equipment required by the staff;
- an average work space of 7.5 square feet [7,000 square centimeters] per researcher;
- researcher tables: should measure 30 inches [76 centimeters] in height; typically a one person table measures a minimum of 36 by 42 inches [91 by 107 centimeters]; a table for more than one person measures a minimum of 48 by 72 inches [1.2 by 1.8 meters];
- research table space for oversized records, such as maps. If oversized material is seldom used, or if space is limited, consider providing several rolling tables that can be placed together to provide larger space when needed;

- reading lamps: lamps on tables must not block the line of sight of the room monitor; and must not exceed the light levels cited in Section 6;
- copier(s): some archives provide for-fee copiers in the reading room. The copiers are located so staff can supervise the copying of archival records.

### 9.12.3 Records Holding Room

Located adjacent to the reading rooms, a records holding room is a secure area that is used to temporarily store records overnight or in advance of a researcher's arrival. The room should have

- the same environmental conditions, fire safety, security, lighting and finishes as the stacks;
- space to store boxes on shelves, book carts holding boxes of records, and any other equipment used by the repository to transport records to the reading rooms;
- records should not be kept longer than 30 days in the records holding room.

### 9.12.4 Finding Aids Room

Though separate spaces for finding aids are becoming less common, some archives will find it useful to provide such a space where visitors and staff can consult computerized or paper finding aids without disrupting the work of other researchers. Sometimes this space is combined with the researcher registration and consultation space.

### 9.12.5 Microfilm Reading Room

The secure and staff monitored reading room that provides micro formats for research should be designed to house and operate the different kinds of equipment needed to access and copy the formats held by the repository. The room should have the capability to lower the lighting levels. Some repositories will provide self-service copies of high-use reference film and fiche in cabinets located in or adjacent to the reading room. Special efforts should be made to minimize dust, including extra housekeeping and additional air filtration.

Many microfilm rooms are being reduced in size or eliminated as microfilm collections become available on-line. Digital workstations are replacing film and fiche readers in many institutions. Each repository must decide on the balance of equipment necessary to serve its collections and researchers.

### 9.12.6 Audiovisual Reading Room

The secure and staff-monitored audiovisual reading room provides the space and specialized equipment to research audiovisual records, including still pictures, motion pictures, videotapes, sound recordings, etc. The room should not have natural lighting and should have light dimming capabilities. Counters, shelves, and cabinets should be flexibly designed to accommodate current and future equipment needs.

## 9.13 PUBLIC SPACES

Public spaces must be welcoming and orient visitors to the archival facility and its components. Public areas must have clear signage. In addition, every public space in the archives should be designed to provide an opportunity for communicating the mission and work of the archives to the public.

### 9.13.1 Lobby

The lobby is the visitor's first impression of the archives facility and the main transitional point among the public spaces. The lobby should be the primary entry for all visitors. Often it is the primary entrance for staff too. It may contain a welcome desk, security screening area and seating for visitors. The lobby should be sized to accommodate the largest group of people anticipated at any one time. Will the archives host school groups? Will the lobby be used by visitors waiting to view the next showing of an orientation film? Will the archives use the lobby for after-hours receptions or conference registration? These answers to these questions will help determine the size of the lobby.

Entrances from the exterior of the building into the lobby should be through two sets of doors separated by a vestibule that provides energy savings and serves as an airlock to keep unconditioned air from entering the building. Shoe cleaning mats in the vestibule will serve to reduce the amount of snow, mud, and dirt that are brought into the building. The lobby is a noisy space and should be well insulated from adjacent quiet spaces, such as training rooms and reading rooms.

Adjacent to the lobby should be

- reading room registration and orientation;
- public lockers/locker room;
- public restrooms;
- meeting or training rooms;
- auditorium;
- exhibit gallery(s).

## 9.13.2 Lockers

Lockers or a locker room should be provided for visitors to store personal materials that are not permitted in the reading rooms. Lockers should be

- adjacent to the lobby and/or the reading rooms;
- secure and well lighted;
- separated from stacks and records use areas—visitors often store food in the lockers;
- close to the visitor eating area;
- a variety of sizes for materials ranging from briefcases and backpacks to the luggage of traveling researchers;

If there is a locker room, provide

- coat rack and umbrella stand;
- table(s) or other flat surface for use when placing items in, or removing items from, lockers;

- bulletin board for announcements, etc.;
- public telephone.

Consider building a larger coat closet adjacent to the locker room with cubbies for book bags and hooks for jackets for visiting school groups. This can also serve as a coat room for archives events. Outfit the door with a combination lock and the coat closet can be secured for groups.

### 9.13.3 Public Restrooms

Restrooms should be accessible from the lobby and close to the public locker room and eating spaces. Restrooms should be convenient to the reading rooms but not located so that researchers can carry documents or books into them. Do not place restrooms over or near records holding or use areas. Restrooms should be equipped with smoke detectors to detect visitor smoking. All archival facilities should be smoke-free environments.

### 9.13.4 Visitor Service Center

This area may serve a variety of functions, such as registering new visitors, orienting first-time visitors, and collecting money for sales of books and/or gift shop items. A visitor service center can be located within the lobby or adjacent to the lobby. Larger archives may divide the functions of this space into a Welcome Desk that is located in the lobby and a Visitor Service area or Registration area adjacent to the lobby or reading rooms.

### 9.13.5 Auditorium/Training/Classroom/Meeting Spaces

Archives should consider carefully what types of public and staff meetings spaces will be required in their facility. Meeting rooms can range from boardroom-sized conference rooms, midsized training or classrooms, to auditoriums that seat hundreds of people. Meeting rooms should be adjacent to the lobby and public restrooms, particularly if they require after-hours access. A large meeting room with movable partitions offers flexibility and serves as a multipurpose space. Some meeting spaces require equipment and storage space for the equipment, including

- televisions;
- projectors;
- computers;
- videoconferencing;
- white boards;
- easels;
- extra tables and chairs.

If food is permitted in meeting spaces, original records should be prohibited and the rooms must be isolated from stacks and other archival spaces.

### 9.13.6 Food Service Area

Food service can consist of a vending operation, self-service eatery, cafeteria, or small restaurant. Any food service area must be located near the lobby and public areas, and away from all stacks, exhibits, and other records use areas. Also, all trash related to the food service area must be located away from stack, exhibits, and other records use areas.

Food service areas should be under slightly negative air pressure to the rest of the building. In addition, vent food service areas directly to the outside rather than into the general building return air system and do not locate those food service vents near air intakes for the rest of the building.

Consider providing an outside eating space for staff and visitors.

### 9.13.7 Gift Shop

The archives gift shop, if one is included, may range in size from a lobby kiosk to a separate room or building. Gift shops are generally located near exhibit spaces and other public areas. The gift shop operation can also be part of welcome desk or visitor orientation center. The gift shop must be able to be secured even if other parts of the building are open. For larger gift shops, provide easy access to the loading dock.

Gift shops require

- separate storage area adjacent to the gift shop for the storage of stock;
- flexible display racks;
- adjustable lighting;
- multiple and accessible electrical outlets;
- cash register and computer equipment;
- manager's office.

## 9.14 EXHIBITION

Exhibition spaces include the exhibit gallery(s), which are public spaces, and the exhibition preparation areas which are restricted to staff. The public exhibit space should be adjacent or near to the public lobby. The archives building can become part of the "exhibit" if windows are provided into key areas not normally accessible to the public, such as laboratories, scanning spaces, and stacks.

Exhibit areas that display original materials should not be exposed to natural light. Ideally exhibit spaces should have a minimum of unencumbered spaces. Display walls should be constructed of materials that permit use of nails. Environmental conditions, security, and materials and finishes must all be considered for archival exhibits. Refer to Sections 3, 5, 6, and 7 for additional guidelines on archival exhibits.

Exhibit preparation space should be large flexible space that includes space for planning, layout work, mat-cutting, exhibit construction, graphics preparation, and storage. Environmental conditions, security, and materials and finishes must all be considered for exhibit prep space. Refer to Sections 3, 5, 6, and 7 for additional guidelines on archival exhibit spaces.

Appendix A

# PROHIBITED MATERIALS

*Michele F. Pacifico*

Below is a list of materials that must never be used in records storage areas or exhibit cases housing original holdings. It is recommended that their use also be prohibited in processing rooms, holding areas, and exhibit galleries.

Asbestos.

Cellulose nitrate-bearing materials, such as cellulose nitrate lacquers, varnishes, and adhesives.

Cellulose diacetate fabrics.

Cellulose acetate fabrics and films.

Polyurethane products including paints, varnishes, and foams.

Acid-curing silicone sealants and adhesives, or similar products that emit acetic acid during cure.

Lead containing materials.

Sulfur-containing materials in any form that could be released as hydrogen sulfide or mercaptans. These include, but are not limited to, vulcanized rubber, animal glue, wool, cadmium sulfide pigments, and disodium phosphate fire retardant treatments.

Magnetic ballasts and their fluorescent lamps unless ultraviolet filtered.

Mercury and metal halide lamps due to their high ultraviolet output.

Modified alkyd paints.

Most pressure-sensitive adhesives and contact cements and adhesives.

Oil-based paints or varnishes.

Unstable chlorine-containing polymers (PVCs), such as polyvinyl chloride and Saran.

Materials that emit formaldehydes (urea/phenol/resorcinol/formaldehyde), as might be found in interior-grade plywood, hardboard, particle board, and plastic laminates.

Products that release ammonia during cure.

Vinyls, including but not limited to unstable chlorine-containing polymers (i.e., polyvinyl chloride and Saran).

Unsealed concrete (due to its production of fine particulate, alkaline dust).

Self-leveling floor compounds.

Oil-based and alkyd resin paints and varnishes, and oil-based caulks and glazing compounds.

Amine-based products.

Biocides.

All combustible furniture.

# Appendix B

# GLOSSARY

*Thomas P. Wilsted*

**ABA.** Architectural Barriers Act.

**ADA.** Americans with Disabilities Act.

**ANSI.** American National Standards Institute.

**approved.** Applies to a material or piece of equipment that has been tested and listed by a nationally or internationally recognized independent testing agency such as Factory Mutual (FM), Underwriter's Laboratories (UL) or that complies with the International Organization for Standardization (ISO) and is accepted for general use.

**ASHRAE.** American Society of Heating, Refrigerating and Air-Conditioning Engineers.

**ballast.** Components that maintain and control electrical current to fluorescent lighting fixtures that prevents tube burn out when starting.

**bay.** A single set of shelves within a row of shelving or a shelving unit.

**building envelope.** The building exterior made up of the walls, roof, windows, doors, floors, and foundation.

**building—fire resistive.** A building in which the structural members, including walls, partitions, columns, floors, and roofs are of non-combustible or of limited combustible materials, and can withstand a fire that completely consumes all combustible contents and finishes without collapse or other structural failure.

**building—nonfire resistive.** A building of the construction type in which the structural members, including walls, partitions, columns, floors, and roofs do not qualify as noncombustible or limited combustible as defined herein.

**candela or candle.** A basic unit of light intensity from which the lumen was developed that is roughly equal to the amount of light from the flame of a single candle.

**clerestories.** Any rows of windows above eye level that allow light into a space. In modern architecture, clerestories provide light without distractions of a view or compromising privacy.

**Color Rendering Index.** A measurement of how well a light source expresses colors, such as a Munsell color chart.

**DALI.** Digital Addressable Lighting Interface is a two way communication system that brings digital technology to lighting.

**daylight factor (DF).** A ratio of the lighting level in a building measured against the simultaneous average outdoor lighting level and expressed as a percentage.

**diffuser.** A glass, plastic, or metal lens designed to distribute light from an electric fixture.

**file processing area.** A room used for preparing records for filing, for retrieving records or filing records into storage.

**finishes.** The final surface treatment or coating on walls, ceilings, floors, or equipment. The material used in surfacing or finishing.

**fire rating.** A construction materials measurement listing the number of hours that a specific item protects building contents from burning or ensures wall stability in a fire.

**fire resistive building.** *see* building—fire resistive

**foot candle.** A level of light from a single candle held one foot from the surface of an item. A foot candle is equivalent to 10.76 lux and one lumen foot -2.

**foundation.** The lower portion of a building wall partly or mostly located below ground level and constructed of concrete, stone, or masonry.

**functional space.** A room or area within an archives in which a specific activity or task occurs.

**glare.** The loss of visual function due to high intensity lighting to which the eye has not yet become adapted.

**HVAC.** An acronym for heating, ventilation, and air-conditioning systems.

**Kelvin (K).** A unit of measurement. One Kelvin degree is equivalent to one Celsius degree. The difference between the two temperature scales: All motion within an atom ceases at zero Kelvin—this point is called absolute zero. Water freezes at zero degrees Celsius, which is approximately 273.16 K.

**LEED** (Leadership in Energy and Environmental Design). A certification system established by the United States Green Building Council that uses a series of credits to designate that a building achieves a range of status levels.

**light damage.** Permanent cumulative injury to archival and special collections caused by exposure to radiation (light).

**light life.** The cumulative light exposure that an item can withstand without significant deterioration.

**lighting.** Quality and quantity of both natural and artificial light within an interior or exterior space.

**locks** (Recommended)

- **Double bolt lock.** A lock that has two horizontal bars that extends from a centrally-mounted case into the jambs on either side of the door. This is mostly used on garage doors.

- **Drop bolt/deadbolt lock.** A lock that uses vertical pins that drop vertically into the receiving plate when the key is turned.

- **Mortise double-cylinder deadbolt lock.** A lock requiring a key on both sides of the door providing greater security than a simple mortise deadbolt lock. Its use may be restricted because of fire regulations.

**locks** (Recommended with reservations)

- **Interconnected lock.** This lock includes both a key-in-the-knob and a cylinder deadbolt often operated by the same key. The danger is that the user may leave the deadbolt unintentionally disengaged, leaving the door unlocked.

- **Mortise or cylinder deadbolt lock.** This lock is operated by a key on the outside and a thumb turn on the inside. While the non-beveled bolt extends one-half inch or more into the door jamb, people often forget to operate the deadbolt when they close the door. When the lock is used as designed, it provides adequate protection against jimmying if the door fits securely into the door jamb.

locks (Not Recommended)

- **Spring bolt lock.** A lock that has either a beveled or square latch that is set by turning a knob. Some have a lock-out feature that keeps the door unlocked at all times. These can also be opened with a credit card or similar device.
- **Key-in-the-knob lock.** The lock includes a beveled latch that extends into the small metal frame on the door jamb. These locks are fairly easy to open with a credit card or similar object.

**lumen.** A metric unit of light measurement. 1 lumen/m$^2$ = 1 foot candle.

**luminance** A measure of reflected light intensity that most closely approximates what the human eye or camera sees. It is usually expressed in candelas per square meter.

**luminaire.** A group of components that together forms a lighting fixture. This may include a lamp (light source), a reflector, an aperture (sometimes with a lens), the fixture encasement (a hard outer to protect and align the electrical components), a ballast, and a socket or other power connection.

**lux.** A metric unit of light. One lux is equal to one lumen per square meter. One lux equals 0.0929 foot candles.

**materials.** Components used in the construction of buildings and products or elements that are incorporated in construction products.

**microwatt per lumen.** A measurement of ultraviolet light energy emitted from a natural or artificial light source.

**mobile shelving.** A system of records storage, also known as track files, compaction files, or movable files, in which sections or rows of shelves are manually or electrically moved on tracks to provide access aisles.

**Munsell value.** The system of color notation developed by A.H. Munsell in 1905 identifies color in terms of three attributes: hue, value, and chroma. The value notation indicates the lightness or darkness of color in relation to a neutral grey scale, which extends from absolute black to absolute white.

**NARA.** National Archives and Records Administration.

**NFPA.** National Fire Protection Association.

**nonfire-resistive building.** *see* building—non-fire resistive.

**open-shelf file equipment.** Any shelving that does not enclose file compartments on six sides.

**OSHA.** Occupational Safety and Health Administration.

**permanent use.** Records storage areas or vaults used for periods of one year or more.

**power limited.** Low voltage devices for fire protection, security, and environmental monitoring as defined in National Fire Protection Association Standard #70 National Electrical Code.

**range.** A length of shelves or bays; also called a row of shelving. Ranges can be single or double faced when two ranges are attached together.

**shall.** A word indicating a mandatory requirement.

**should.** A word indicating a recommendation that is advised but not required.

**stack.** A records storage area.

**temporary use.** Records storage area or vaults used for a period of less than one year.

**ultraviolet (UV) light.** Invisible short wavelength light measured from 200 to 400 nanometers that cause paper deterioration. Normal glass filters radiation shorter than 330 nanometers and additional filters are required for UV light in the 330 to 400-nanometer spectrum.

**vapor barrier.** A waterproof membrane such as plastic or foil used to seal building foundations and exterior walls from water or moisture penetration.

**vault.** A fire resistive enclosure designed and equipped to minimize the potential of a fire originating within and preventing a fire occurring outside from penetrating the enclosure. Vaults are defined as:

- "Standard" having a maximum size of 15,000 cubic feet [426 cubic meters];

- "Oversized" 15,000 cubic feet [426 cubic meters] to a maximum 25,000 cubic feet [710 cubic meters].

**vault door.** A door tested and listed by a nationally or internationally recognized, independent testing agency such as Factory Mutual (FM), Underwriters Laboratories (UL) or complying with the requirements of the International Organization for Standardization (ISO).

**volatile organic compound (VOC).** Any organic compound that evaporates readily into the atmosphere. VOCs contribute significantly to archival deterioration and are found in construction materials, sealants, carpets, ceiling and wall finishes, paints, and furniture.

**wet weight:** The gross weight of a water saturated vault whose contents include but are not limited to artifacts, documents, manuscripts and other paper materials. The wet weight of paper records is approximately 2.4 times the dry weight. Dry correspondence files weigh approximately 30 pounds per square feet [480 kilograms per square meters].

# Appendix C

# BIBLIOGRAPHY

*Thomas P. Wilsted*

## ALPHABETICAL BIBLIOGRAPHY

ACRL/RBMS Security Committee. *Guidelines for the Security of Rare Book, Manuscript, and Other Special Collections*. Chicago: Association of College and Research Libraries, 1999.

American Congress on Surveying & Mapping, *Minimum Standard Detail Requirements for ALTA/ACSM Land Title Surveys as Adopted by American Land Title Association and National Society of Professional Surveyors*. Gaithersburg, Md., 2005.

The American Institute of Architects. *Security Planning and Design: A Guide for Architects and Repository Design Professionals*. Joseph A. Demkin, ed. Hoboken, N.J.: John Wiley and Sons, Inc., 2003.

American Library Association. Association of College and Research Libraries. "Guidelines Regarding Thefts in Libraries." Chicago: 2006. See http://www.ala.org/ala/acrl/acrlstandards/guidelinesregardingthefts.htm.

American National Standards Institute. ANSI Standard A250.4. *Test Procedure and Acceptance Criteria for—Physical Endurance for Steel Doors, Frames, Frame Anchors and Hardware Reinforcings*. Washington, D.C.: American National Standards Institute, 2001.

American National Standards Institute. ANSI Standard A250.8. *Recommended Specifications for Standard Steel Doors and Frames.* Washington, D.C.: American National Standards Institute, 2003.

American Society of Heating, Refrigerating and Air-Conditioning Engineers. *ASHRAE Handbook: Heating, Ventilating and Air-Conditioning Applications.* Chapter 21: Museums, Libraries and Archives Design, Atlanta, Ga.: American Society of Heating and Air-Conditioning Engineers, 2003.

American Society of Heating, Refrigerating and Air-Conditioning Engineers. *Control of Gaseous Indoor Contaminants.* Atlanta, Ga.: American Society of Heating and Air-Conditioning Engineers, 2003.

ASIS International. *Facilities Physical Security Measures Guideline.* Draft. 2008. See: http://www.asisonline.org.

ANSI/ASME A17.1-2007—*Safety Code for Elevators and Escalators* (Bi-national standard with CSA B44-07). New York: American Society of Mechanical Engineers, 2007.

Archives New Zealand. *Storage Standard.* Wellington, New Zealand, 2007. See: http://www.archives.govt.nz.

Artim, Nick. *Introduction to Fire Detection, Alarm, and Automatic Sprinklers.* Andover, Mass.: Northeast Document Conservation Center, 1995.

Baril, Paul. *A Fire Protection Primer.* Ottawa: Canadian Conservation Institute, 1995.

Boyce, P. R. *Human Factors in Lighting.* London: Taylor & Francis Group, 2003.

British Standards Institute, *BS 5454: Recommendations for the Storage and Exhibition of Archival Documents.* London: British Standards Institute, 2000.

British Standards Institute. *Recommendations for the Storage and Exhibition of Archival Documents.* BSI 04-2000, Prepared by Technical Subcommittee IDT/2/9, 2000.

Brown, G. Z. and Mark DeKay. *Sun, Wind & Light: Architectural Design Strategies.* New York: John Wiley and Sons, 2001.

Brown, G. Z., John S. Reynolds, and M. Susan Ubbelohde. *Inside Out: Design Procedures for Passive Environmental Technologies.* New York: John Wiley and Sons, 1982.

Council for Museums, Archives and Libraries. *Security in Museums, Archives and Libraries.* 2nd ed. London: Council for Museums, Archives and Libraries, 2003.

Crewes, Patricia Cox. "A Comparison of Selected UV Filtering Materials for the Reduction of Fading." *Journal of the American Institute for Conservation.* 28:2: Article 5, (pp. 117–125).

Cuttle, C. *Lighting by Design.* Oxford: Architectural Press, Elsevier Science, 2003.

Demkin, Joseph A., Ed., *Security Planning and Design: A Guide for Architects and Building Design Professionals.* Hoboken, N.J.: John Wiley and Sons, 2004.

Eccleston, Charles H. *The NEPA Planning Process: A Comprehensive Guide with Emphasis on Efficiency.* New York: John Wiley and Sons, Inc., 1999.

Erhardt, L. *The Right Light.* New York: IESNA, 1995.

Environmental Protection Agency. *Mold Resources.* See: http://www.epa.gov.

Federal Emergency Management Agency. *Communicating with Owners and Managers of New Buildings on Earthquake Risk.* FEMA Report 342. Washington, D.C.: FEMA, n.d.

Federal Emergency Management Agency. *Designing for Earthquakes: A Manual for Architects.* Washington, D.C.: FEMA, 2006 See: http://www.fema.gov/library.

Federal Emergency Management Agency. *Design Guide for Improving Critical Facility Safety from Flooding and High Winds.* FEMA Report 543. Washington, D.C.: FEMA, n.d.

Feller, R. "Control of Deteriorating Effects of Light on Museum Objects: Heating Effects of Illumination by Incandescent Lamps." *Museum News,* Technical Supplement, May 1968.

Fennelly, Lawrence J. *Museum, Archive and Library Security*, Boston: Butterworths, 1983.

Flynn, J. E., J. A. Kremers, et al. *Architectural Interior Systems: Lighting, Acoustics, Air Conditioning.* New York: Van Nostrand Reinhold, 1992.

Glaser, Mary Todd. "Protecting Paper and Book Collections during Exhibition." *Northeast Document Conservation Center Preservation Leaflets*, Number 2.5. Andover, Mass.: Northeast Document Conservation Center, 2007.

Hatchfield, Pamela. *Pollutants in the Museum Environment: Practical Strategies for Problem Solving in Design, Exhibition, Storage.* London: Archetype Publications, 2002.

Hollow Metal Manufacturers Association (A Division of NAAMM). ANSI/NAAMM HMMA 861-00. *Guide Specifications for Commercial Hollow Metal Doors and Frames.* Glen Ellyn, Ill.: National Association of Architectural Metal Manufacturers, 2000.

Hollow Metal Manufacturers Association (A Division of NAAMM). ANSI/NAAMM HMMA 862-03. *Guide Specifications for Commercial Security Hollow Metal Doors and Frames.* Glen Ellyn, Ill.: National Association of Architectural Metal Manufacturers, 2003.

Illuminating Engineering Society of North America. *Daylighting* (Recommended Practice RP-5-79). New York: IESNA, n.d.

Illuminating Engineering Society of North America. *Educational Facilities Lighting* (Recommended Practice RP-3-88). New York: IESNA, n.d.

Illuminating Engineering Society of North America. *Industrial Lighting* (Recommended Practice RP-7-91). New York: IESNA, n.d.

Illuminating Engineering Society of North America. *Museum and Art Gallery Lighting: A Recommended Practice.* New York: IESNA, 1996.

Illuminating Engineering Society of North America. *Office Lighting.* New York: IESNA, n.d.

Illuminating Engineering Society of North America. *The IESNA Lighting Handbook.* New York: IESNA, 2000.

International Organization for Standardization, *ISO 11799: Information and Documentation—Documentation Storage Requirements for*

*Archive and Library Materials.* Geneva, Switzerland: International Organization for Standardization, 2003.

International Organization for Standardization, *ISO 15489: Information and Documentation—Records Management—Part 1: General and Part 2: Guidelines.* Geneva, Switzerland: International Organization for Standardization, 2001.

Keller, Steven R. *Conducting the Physical Survey.* Deltona, Fla.: Steven Keller and Associates, Inc., 1988.

Lam, W. M. C. *Perception and Lighting as Formgivers for Architecture.* New York: McGraw-Hill Book Company, 1997.

Leighton, Philip and David C. Weber. *Planning Academic and Research Libraries.* Chicago: American Library Association Editions, 2000.

Michalski, S. *Artifact and Lighting: Visibility vs. Vulnerability.* Ottawa: Canadian Conservation Institute, 1997.

Michalski, Stefan. *Guidelines for Humidity and Temperature for Canadian Archives.* Ottawa: Canadian Conservation Institute, Technical Bulletin 23, 2000.

Michalski, Stefan. *Research Project: Light Damage Calculator and Database.* Ottawa: Canadian Conservation Institute, 2004.

National Air Filtration Association. *NAFA Guide to Air Filtration.* 3rd ed., Virginia Beach, Va.: National Air Filtration Association, 2001

National Archives. *Standard for Record Repositories.* London: The National Archives, 2004.

National Archives and Records Administration. *Architecture and Design Standards for Presidential Libraries.* College Park, Md.: NARA, 2007.

National Archives and Records Administration. *Architectural and Design Standards for Regional Archives.* College Park, Md.: NARA, 2000.

National Archives and Records Administration. *Archival Storage Standards, NARA 1571*, College Park, Md.: NARA, 2002.

National Archives and Records Administration. "Archives II, Using Technology to Safeguard Archival Records." *Technical Information Paper Number 1.* College Park, Md.: NARA, 1997.

National Archives and Records Administration. "NARA's Specifications for Housing Enclosures for Archival Records, 1991–1996." See: http://www.archives.gov.

National Archives and Records Administration. "Products Tested by the NARA Research and Testing Laboratory (1991–present)." See: http://www.archives.gov.

National Fire Protection Association. *NFPA 78, Lighting Protection Code.* Quincy, Mass.: National Fire Protection Association, 1989.

National Fire Protection Association. *NFPA 232 Standard for Protection of Records 2007 Edition.* Quincy, Mass.: National Fire Protection Association, 2007.

National Fire Protection Association. *NFPA 909 Code for the Protection of Cultural Resources—Museums, Libraries and Places of Worship.* Quincy, Mass.: National Fire Protection Association, 2005.

National Fire Protection Association. *NFPA 914 Code for the Fire Protection of Historic Structures.* Quincy, Mass.: National Fire Protection Association, 2007.

National Information Standards Organization. *Environmental Conditions for Exhibiting Library and Archival Materials.* Bethesda, Md.: NISO Press, 2001.

National Information Standards Organization. *Single-tier Steel Bracket Library Shelving.* Bethesda, Md.: NISO Press, 1994.

National Research Council. *Preservation of Historical Records.* Washington, D.C.: National Academy Press, 1986.

Ogden, Sherelyn. "Storage Furniture: A Brief Review of Current Options." *Northeast Document Conservation Center Preservation Leaflets,* Number 4.2. Andover, Mass.: Northeast Document Conservation Center, 2007.

Society of Archivists, Irish Region. *Standards for Development of Archives Services in Ireland.* Dublin, Ireland: Society of Archivists Irish Region, 1997.

Tétreault, Jean. *Airborne Pollutants in Museums, Galleries and Archives: Risk Assessment, Control Strategies, and Preservation Management.* Ottawa: Canadian Conservation Institute, 2004.

Tétreault, Jean. *Guidelines for Selecting Materials for Exhibit, Storage and Transportation*. Ottawa: Canadian Conservation Institute, 1993.

Tétreault, Jean. *Guidelines for Selecting and Using Coatings*. Ottawa: Canadian Conservation Institute, 2002.

Tétreault, Jean. *Measuring Acidity of Volatile Products*. Ottawa: Canadian Conservation Institute, 1992.

Thomson, G. *The Museum Environment*. 3rd, rev. ed. London: Butterworth, 1986.

Trinkaus-Randall, Gregor. *Protecting Your Collections: A Manual of Archival Security*. Chicago: Society of American Archivists, 1995.

United States Access Board. *ADA and ABA Accessibility Guidelines for Buildings and Facilities*. Washington, D.C.: 2004.

Walter, Henry. "Notes on Conservation Lab Design," January 1992. See: http://www.palimpsest.stanford.edu.

Wilson, William K. *Environmental Guidelines for the Storage of Paper Records*. Bethesda, Md.: NISO Press, 1995.

Wilsted, Thomas P. *Planning New and Remodeled Archival Facilities*. Chicago: Society of American Archivists. 2006.

United States Access Board. *ADA and ABA Accessibility Guidelines for Buildings and Facilities*. Washington, D.C.: 2004.

## SUBJECT BIBLIOGRAPHY

### International Facilities Standards

International Organization for Standardization. *ISO 11799: Information and Documentation—Documentation Storage Requirements for Archive and Library Materials*. Geneva, Switzerland: International Organization for Standardization, 2003.

International Organization for Standardization, *ISO 15489: Information and Documentation—Records Management—Part 1: General and Part 2: Guidelines*. Geneva, Switzerland: International Organization for Standardization, 2001.

## United States Facilities Standards

National Information Standards Organization. *Environmental Conditions for Exhibiting Library and Archival Material.* Bethesda, Md.: NISO Press, 2001.

## Other National Standards

Archives New Zealand. *Storage Standard.* Wellington, New Zealand: 2007. See: http://www.archives.govt.nz/continuum/documents/publications/s2.

British Standards Institute. *BS 5454: Recommendations for the Storage and Exhibition of Archival Documents.* London: British Standards Institute, 2000.

National Archives. *Standard for Record Repositories.* London: The National Archives, 2004.

Society of Archivists, Irish Region. *Standards for Development of Archives Services in Ireland,* Dublin, Ireland: Society of Archivists Irish Region, 1997.

## United States Organizational Facilities Standards

National Archives and Records Administration. *Architecture and Design Standards for Presidential Libraries.* College Park, Md.: NARA, 2007.

National Archives and Records Administration. *Architectural and Design Standards for Regional Archives,* College Park, Md.: NARA, 2000.

National Archives and Records Administration. *Archival Storage Standards, NARA 1571,* College Park, Md.: NARA, 2002.

## United States Specialized Standards—Building Environment

American Society of Heating, Refrigerating and Air-Conditioning Engineers. *ASHRAE Handbook: Heating, Ventilating and Air-Conditioning Applications.* Chapter 21: Museums, Libraries and Archives Design, Atlanta, Ga.: American Society of Heating and Air-Conditioning Engineers, 2003.

American Society of Heating, Refrigerating and Air-Conditioning Engineers. *Control of Gaseous Indoor Contaminants*. Atlanta, Ga.: American Society of Heating and Air-Conditioning Engineers, 2003.

Environmental Protection Agency. *Mold Resources*. See: http://www.epa.gov/iaq/molds.

Hatchfield, Pamela. *Pollutants in the Museum Environment: Practical Strategies for Problem Solving in Design, Exhibition, Storage*. London: Archetype Publications, 2002.

Michalski, Stefan. *Guidelines for Humidity and Temperature for Canadian Archives*. Ottawa: Canadian Conservation Institute, Technical Bulletin 23, 2000.

National Air Filtration Association. *NAFA Guide to Air Filtration*. 3rd ed., Virginia Beach, Va.: National Air Filtration Association, 2001.

National Archives and Records Administration. *Archival Storage Standards, NARA 1571*. College Park, Md.: NARA, 2002.

National Research Council. *Preservation of Historical Records*. Washington, D.C.: National Academy Press, 1986.

Tétreault, Jean. *Airborne Pollutants in Museums, Galleries and Archives: Risk Assessment, Control Strategies, and Preservation Management*. Ottawa: Canadian Conservation Institute, 2004.

## United States Specialized Standards—Building Site

American Congress on Surveying & Mapping. *Minimum Standard Detail Requirements For ALTA/ACSM Land Title Surveys as Adopted by American Land Title Association and National Society of Professional Surveyors*. Gaithersburg, Md., 2005.

Eccleston, Charles H. *The NEPA Planning Process: A Comprehensive Guide with Emphasis on Efficiency*. New York: John Wiley and Sons, Inc., 1999.

Federal Emergency Management Agency. *Communicating with Owners and Managers of New Buildings on Earthquake Risk*. FEMA Report 342. Washington, D.C.: FEMA, n.d.

Federal Emergency Management Agency. *Designing for Earthquakes: A Manual for Architects.* Washington, D.C.: FEMA, 2006 See: http://www.fema.gov/library.

Federal Emergency Management Agency. *Design Guide for Improving Critical Facility Safety from Flooding and High Winds.* FEMA Report 543. Washington, D.C.: FEMA, n.d.

United States Access Board *ADA and ABA Accessibility Guidelines for Buildings and Facilities.* Washington, D.C.: 2004.

## United States Specialized Standards—Fire Protection

Artim, Nick. *Introduction to Fire Detection, Alarm, and Automatic Sprinklers.* Andover, Mass.: Northeast Document Conservation Center, 1995.

Baril, Paul. *A Fire Protection Primer.* Ottawa: Canadian Conservation Institute 1995.

National Fire Protection Association. *NFPA 232 Standard for Protection of Records 2007 Edition.* Quincy, Mass.: National Fire Protection Association, 2007.

National Fire Protection Association. *NFPA 909 Code for the Protection of Cultural Resources—Museums, Libraries and Places of Worship 2005 Edition.* Quincy, Mass.: National Fire Protection Association, 2005.

National Fire Protection Association. *NFPA 914 Code for the Fire Protection of Historic Structures.* Quincy, Mass.: National Fire Protection Association, 2007.

National Archives and Records Administration. *Architecture and Design Standards for Presidential Libraries.* College Park, Md.: NARA, 2007.

National Archives and Records Administration. *Architectural and Design Standards for Regional Archives.* College Park, Md.: NARA, 2000.

National Archives and Records Administration. *Archival Storage Standards, NARA 1571,* College Park, Md.: NARA, 2002.

## Specialized Standards—Functional Spaces

ACRL/RBMS Security Committee. *Guidelines for the Security of Rare Book, Manuscript, and Other Special Collections*. Chicago: Association of College and Research Libraries, 1999.

ANSI/ASME A17.1-2007—*Safety Code for Elevators and Escalators* (Bi-national standard with CSA B44-07). New York: American Society of Mechanical Engineers, 2007.

Walter Henry. "Notes on Conservation Lab Design." January 1992. See: http://palimpsest.stanford.edu/byauth/henry/labdesgn.html.

National Archives and Records Administration. *Architecture and Design Standards for Presidential Libraries*. College Park, Md.: NARA, 2007.

National Archives and Records Administration. *Architectural and Design Standards for Regional Archives*. College Park, Md.: NARA, 2000.

Wilsted, Thomas P. *Planning New and Remodeled Archival Facilities*. Chicago: Society of American Archivists, 2006.

## Specialized Standards—Lighting

Boyce, P. R. *Human Factors in Lighting*. London: Taylor & Francis Group, 2003.

Brown, G. Z., and Mark DeKay. *Sun, Wind & Light: Architectural Design Strategies*. New York: John Wiley and Sons, 2001.

Brown, G. Z., John S. Reynolds, and M. Susan Ubbelohde. *Inside Out: Design Procedures for Passive Environmental Technologies*. New York: John Wiley and Sons, 1982.

Crewes, Patricia Cox. "A Comparison of Selected UV Filtering Materials for the Reduction of Fading." *Journal of the American Institute for Conservation*. 28:2: Article 5, (pp. 117–125).

Cuttle, C. *Lighting by Design*. Oxford: Architectural Press, Elsevier Science, 2003.

Erhardt, L. *The Right Light*. New York: IESNA, 1995.

Feller, R. "Control of Deteriorating Effects of Light on Museum Objects: Heating Effects of Illumination by Incandescent Lamps." *Museum News*. Technical Supplement, May 1968.

Flynn, J. E., J. A. Kremers, et al. *Architectural Interior Systems: Lighting, Acoustics, Air Conditioning*. New York: Van Nostrand Reinhold, 1992.

Illuminating Engineering Society of North America. *Daylighting* (Recommended Practice RP-5-79). New York: IESNA. n.d.

Illuminating Engineering Society of North America. *Educational Facilities Lighting* (Recommended Practice RP-3-88). New York: IESNA, n.d.

Illuminating Engineering Society of North America. *Industrial Lighting* (Recommended Practice RP-7-91), New York: IESNA, n.d.

Illuminating Engineering Society of North America. *Museum and Art Gallery Lighting: A Recommended Practice*. New York: IESNA, 1996.

Illuminating Engineering Society of North America. *Office Lighting*. New York: IESNA, n.d.

Illuminating Engineering Society of North America. *The IESNA Lighting Handbook*. New York: IESNA, 2000.

Lam, W. M. C. *Perception and Lighting as Formgivers for Architecture*. New York, McGraw-Hill Book Company, 1997.

Michalski, S. *Artifact and Lighting: Visibility vs. Vulnerability*. Ottawa: Canadian Conservation Institute, 1997.

Michalski, Stefan. *Research Project: Light Damage Calculator and Database*. Ottawa: Canadian Conservation Institute, 2004.

National Fire Protection Association. *NFPA 78, Lighting Protection Code*. Quincy, Mass.: National Fire Protection Association, 1989.

Thomson, G. *The Museum Environment*. 3rd, rev. ed. London: Butterworth, 1986.

## Specialized Standards—Materials and Finishes

Glaser, Mary Todd. "Protecting Paper and Book Collections during Exhibition." *Northeast Document Conservation Center Preservation*

*Leaflets*, Number 2.5. Andover, Mass.: Northeast Document Conservation Center, 2007.

National Archives and Records Administration. *Architecture and Design Standards for Presidential Libraries.* College Park, Md.: NARA, 2007.

National Archives and Records Administration. *Architectural and Design Standards for Regional Archives*, College Park, Md.: NARA, 2000.

National Archives and Records Administration. "Archives II, Using Technology to Safeguard Archival Records." *Technical Information Paper Number 1.* College Park, Md.: NARA, 1997.

National Archives and Records Administration. "NARA's Specifications for Housing Enclosures for Archival Records, 1991–1996." See: http://www.archives.gov.

National Archives and Records Administration. "Products Tested by the NARA Research and Testing Laboratory (1991–present)." See: http://www.archives.gov.

Ogden, Sherelyn. "Storage Furniture: A Brief Review of Current Options." *Northeast Document Conservation Center Preservation Leaflets,* Number 4.2. Andover, Mass.: Northeast Document Conservation Center, 2007.

Tétreault, Jean. *Guidelines for Selecting Materials for Exhibit, Storage and Transportation.* Ottawa: Canadian Conservation Institute, 1993.

Tétreault, Jean. *Guidelines for Selecting and Using Coatings.* Ottawa: Canadian Conservation Institute, 2002.

Tétreault, Jean. *Measuring Acidity of Volatile Products.* Ottawa: Canadian Conservation Institute, 1992.

## Specialized Standards—Security

The American Institute of Architects. *Security Planning and Design: A Guide for Architects and Repository Design Professionals.* Joseph A. Demkin, ed. Hoboken: John Wiley and Sons, Inc., 2003.

American Library Association. Association of College and Research Libraries. "Guidelines Regarding Thefts in Libraries." 2006. See: http://www.ala.org/ala/acrl/acrlstandards/guidelinesregardingthefts.htm.

American National Standards Institute. ANSI Standard A250.4. *Test Procedure and Acceptance Criteria for—Physical Endurance for Steel Doors, Frames, Frame Anchors and Hardware Reinforcings.* Washington, D.C.: American National Standards Institute, 2001.

American National Standards Institute. ANSI Standard A250.8. *Recommended Specifications for Standard Steel Doors and Frames* Washington, D.C.: American National Standards Institute, 2003.

ASIS International. *Facilities Physical Security Measures Guideline.* Draft. 2008. See: http://www.asisonline.org.

British Standards Institute. *Recommendations for the Storage and Exhibition of Archival Documents, BSI 04-2000,* Prepared by Technical Subcommittee IDT/2/9, 2000.

Council for Museums, Archives and Libraries. *Security in Museums, Archives and Libraries.* 2nd ed. London: Council for Museums, Archives and Libraries, 2003.

Demkin, Joseph A., ed., *Security Planning and Design; A Guide for Architects and Building Design Professionals,* Hoboken, N.J.: John Wiley and Sons, 2004.

Fennelly, Lawrence J. *Museum, Archive and Library Security,* Boston: Butterworths, 1983.

Hollow Metal Manufacturers Association (A Division of NAAMM). ANSI/NAAMM HMMA 861-00. *Guide Specifications for Commercial Hollow Metal Doors and Frames.* Glen Ellyn, Ill: National Association of Architectural Metal Manufacturers, 2000.

Hollow Metal Manufacturers Association (A Division of NAAMM). ANSI/NAAMM HMMA 862-03. *Guide Specifications for Commercial Security Hollow Metal Doors and Frames.* Glen Ellyn, Ill: National Association of Architectural Metal Manufacturers, 2003.

International Organization for Standardization. *ISO 11799: Information and Documentation—Documentation Storage Requirements for Archive and Library Materials,* Geneva, Switzerland: International Organization for Standardization, 2003.

National Archives. *Standard for Record Repositories.* Richmond, England: The National Archives, 2004.

National Archives and Records Administration. *Architecture and Design Standards for Presidential Libraries*. College Park, Md.: NARA, 2007.

Society of Archivists, Irish Region, *Standards for Development of Archives Services in Ireland,* Dublin, Ireland: Society of Archivists Irish Region, 1997.

Trinkaus-Randall, Gregor. *Protecting Your Collections: A Manual of Archival Security.* Chicago: Society of American Archivists, 1995.

## Specialized Standards—Storage Equipment

British Standards Institute, *BS 5454: Recommendations for the Storage and Exhibition of Archival Documents*, London: British Standards Institute, 2000.

National Archives and Records Administration. *Architecture and Design Standards for Presidential Libraries*. College Park, Md.: NARA, 2007.

National Archives and Records Administration. *Architectural and Design Standards for Regional Archives*. College Park, Md.: NARA, 2000.

National Archives and Records Administration. *Archival Storage Standards, NARA 1571*, College Park, Md.: NARA, 2002.

National Archives and Records Administration. "Archives II, Using Technology to Safeguard Archival Records." *Technical Information Paper Number 1*. College Park, Md.: NARA, 1997.

Ogden, Sherelyn. "Storage Furniture: A Brief Review of Current Options." *Northeast Document Conservation Center Preservation Leaflets,* Number 4.2. Andover, Mass: Northeast Document Conservation Center, 2007.

Tétreault, Jean. *Guidelines for Selecting Materials for Exhibit, Storage and Transportation*. Ottawa: Canadian Conservation Institute. 1993.

Wilsted, Thomas P. *Planning New and Remodeled Archival Facilities*. Chicago: Society of American Archivists. 2006.

# INDEX

**Boldface indicates figures and tables**

ABA. *See* Architectural Barriers Act
absorption materials, 121
access
    at building site, 9
    for emergency vehicles, 17
    to mechanical systems, 28
    to reading rooms, 65, 146
    to stacks, 31, 59
Accessibility Guidelines
    (ADA-ABA), 17
acclimatization
    of building materials, 98
    of cold records, 32, 33
    of exhibit cases, 112
acetate-base photographic film,
    34–35
acetate magnetic tape, 35
acetic acid, **42**, 99, 114
acrylic, 105, 115
    furniture, **109**, 110
activated carbon, 121
ADA. *See* Americans with
    Disabilities Act
adhesives, 96, 115
    carpet, 108, 119
    wood, 112

airborne particulates, 40
air conditioning. *See also* heating,
    ventilation, and air-conditioning
    (HVAC) systems
    acclimatization and, 98
    filtration in, 39–42, 121
    main shut-off for, 50
air intakes, 28
air pressure
    positive and negative, 27, 134,
    152
aisles, 127–128
alarms
    on doors, 70
    microwave, 71
    silent, 72
    in stacks, 64
    on windows, 69
alkyd paints, 102, 109, 117, 119
aluminum, 106
    anodized, **104**, 104–105, **109**
    furniture, 110, 117
American Congress on Surveying
    and Mapping, 11
American Land Title Association, 11

American National Standards
   Institute (ANSI)
   ANSI/UL 155, *Tests for Fire
   Resistance of Vault and File
   Room Doors*, 49
   MH28.2, *Specifications for the
   Design and Testing of Metal-
   Wood Shelving*, 124
American Society of Heating,
   Refrigerating and Air-
   Conditioning Engineers
   ASHRAE 90.1, 24
Americans with Disabilities Act
   (ADA), 17, 19, 45
amine-based products, 99
animals, 25
ANSI. *See* American National
   Standards Institute
archeological assessment, 12–13
Architectural Barriers Act (ABA), 17
archival environments
   air filtration in, 39–41
   building construction and,
   21–23
   criteria for, **36**, **37**
   electronic controls for, 43
   for electronic records, 35–36
   for film-based records, 34–35
   fluctuations in, 38–39
   mechanical systems for, 37–38
   for paper-based records, 32–34
   rationale for, 31–32
   recommendations for, **42**
asbestos, 96, 103
auditorium/training/meeting rooms
   design criteria for, 145, 151–152
   environmental criteria for, **37**
   lighting in, **81**, 90–91

bamboo flooring, **99**, 101, **107**, 109
below ground construction, 20–21,
   21–23
biocide, 99
biometric identification, 69

bird netting, 136
boxes, dimensions of, 130
building codes, 13
   for fire safety, 45, 46–47
   life safety codes, 19, 20, 45,
   126, 127
building construction
   acclimatization and, 98
   archeological work and, 12–13
   building envelope in, 23, 27
   building structure in, 23–26
   commissioning and, 30
   electrical systems in, 29–30
   environmental issues in, 21–23
   exterior openings in, 25
   fire codes and, 46–47
   fire safety in, 24, 47–49
   floors in, 24
   framing in, 23
   insulation in, 23–24
   isolation of fire and smoke in,
   47
   location and ground level of,
   20–21
   materials in, 24, 97–98
   mechanical systems in, 27–29
   pools and fountains in, 25
   rationale for, 19–20
   roof in, 25–26
   seismic considerations in, 24
building site
   archeological assessment of,
   12–13
   emergency vehicles and, 17
   evaluation of, 10–13
   geotechnical investigation of, 11
   historic preservation and, 13–14
   landscaping at, 14–15
   Leadership in Energy and
   Environmental Design (LEED),
   14
   parking and public access at, 17
   rationale for, 7
   security risk assessment of, 12

## Index

selection of, 7–10
site design at, 13–17
size of building site, 9–10
survey of, 11
utilities and, 15–17

cabinets, 104–106
call boxes, manual fire alarm, 52
Canadian Conservation Institute, 120
carpet, **99**, 101, **107**, 108
   in reading rooms, 119
   in stacks, **104**, 105
Carpet and Rug Institute Indoor Air Quality Standards (Green Label Program), 108, 119
carriages, for mobile shelving, 126
carts, 106, 108
caulks, 103
cave storage, 21–23
CD and DVD records, 36
ceilings
   materials and finishes for, 102, 109, 116–117
   in reading rooms, 119
cellulose acetate, 40
cellulose nitrate, 39, 96, 115
chlorine polymers (PVC), 96
chrome-plated steel, 104, **104**
classrooms. *See* auditorium/training/meeting rooms
clean agent systems, for fire suppression, 55
closed-access areas, 61
closed-circuit television (CCTV), 72–73
cold storage
   environmental criteria for, **36**
   fire suppression in, 55
   lighting levels in, **80**, 83
   shelving in, 131
collections
   access to, 66
   protection of, 19
color, lighting and, 84, 86, 93
commissioning, 30
   Committee on the Preservation of Historical Records, **42**
compact fluorescent lamps, 77
   compact mobile shelving systems, 123–124
   criteria for, 125–126
   fire suppression systems in, 54–55
   materials and finishes for, 106
computer room, **81**, 92, 143
concrete
   floors, 99, **99**, **107**, 108, 116
   sealing and coating, 21, 97, 99
condensation, on cold records, 33
conduit, 48
   conference rooms. *See* auditorium/training/meeting rooms
copy/fax/mail areas, 145
cork flooring, **99**, 101, **107**, 109
corridors, **81**, 93, 138
costs, of lighting, 76–78
cotton, undyed, 114, **114**
Council of State Archivists (CoSA), 5
countertops, 117–118

daylight, 76, 77
desiccants, 32
dew point, 32
Digital Addressable Lighting Interface (DALI) lighting systems, 82, 90
digital records (hard drives), 36
direct expansion cooling (dx), 38
DL fixtures, 93
doors
   fire rating of, 49, 61–62
   intruder detection systems on, 70
   in laboratories, 139
   of loading dock, 136

lobby, 150
　for reading rooms, 147
　in reading rooms, 147
　security of exterior, 60–61
　of stacks, 49
drainage
　in floors, 29
　in laboratories, 139
　at loading dock, 134
　of roof, 16, 25
　security of, 59
　storm drains and, 16
drop ceilings, 102
dry-pipe sprinkler systems, 53, 54
dual technology sensors, 72
ducts, 50
dust control, 40
　in below ground and cave construction, 22
　concrete and, 99
　flooring and, 101
　in microfilm reading rooms, 149
dust filtration, criteria for, **36–37**

Early Suppression Fast Response (ESFR) sprinklers, 55
economics of lighting, 76–78
electrical systems, 29–30
　security of, 59
electric power
　at building site, 16
　in computer rooms, 143
　in laboratories, 140
electronic control systems
　for access, 68–70
　in cold storage, 32
　in HVAC systems, 43
electronic digital lock, 68
electronic records, 35–36, **36**, 39
elevators, 49
　freight, 138
　lighting in, **81**, 93–94
　passenger, 139
emergency exits, 61, 62

emergency power system, 20, 29–30
　computer room and, 143
　electronic locks and, 63, 68
emergency services
　in cave construction, 22–23
　in site selection, 8
　vehicular access for, 17
enamel paints, 104, 106, 107
　environmental issues. *See* archival environments
epoxy, 99, 100, 110–111, 118
equipment
　in laboratories, 141–142
　placement on roof, 26
　redundancy of, 29
evacuation, 9
exhibit areas
　design criteria for, 153
　environment in, 34, **36**, 41
　fire suppression in, 55
　lighting in, **80**, 86–87
　materials and finishes in, 107, **107**
　security of, 66–67
　windows in, 59
exhibit cases, 112–115
exterior areas, **81**, 94
eyewashes, 139

fabrics, 112
　in exhibit cases, 113–114, **114**
　in furniture, 117
　in shelving and cabinets, **104**, 105
　in stacks, **104**, 105
felt, 115
fiberglass, 103
fiber optic lighting, 87
film-based records, 34–35, **36**, 39
filters, in lighting, 77
finding aids room, 89, 148
fire code, 61
fire department, 17, 60
　response in remote areas, 22–23

standpipes and hoses for, 52
fire detection and alarm system, 45, 51–52
fire extinguishers, 52, 107
fire mode in compact shelving, 54
fire protection
  building construction and, 24, 46–47
  electrical systems, 50–51
  fire retardant fabric and, 114, **114**
  landscape design and, 15
  low oxygen systems for, 55–56
  mechanical systems and, 49–50
  rationale for, 45–46
  risk assessment for, 46
  stack construction and, 47–49
fire rating of doors, 61–62
fire suppression
  automatic systems for, 53–55
  low oxygen systems for, 55–56
  manual systems for, 52
flat files, 130–131
flooding. *See also* water intrusion
  in cave storage, 21
  fire fighting and, 20
floodplain, 10
floors and flooring
  bamboo, **99**, 101
  carpet, **99**, 101
  in computer rooms, 143
  concrete, 99, **99**, **107**, 108, 116
  construction of, 24
  cork, **99**, 101
  drains in, 29
  in laboratories, 139
  loading of, 24, 124
  materials and finishes for, 108–109
  in reading rooms, 119
  in stacks, 98–101, **99**
  in temporary storage areas, **107**
  tile, **99**, 101, **107**, 109, 116

fluctuations, in climate conditions, 31, 38–39
fluorescent lighting, 78
foam, in display cases, 115
food service/lunchroom
  design criteria for, 144–145, 152
  environmental criteria for, **37**
  lighting in, **81**, 91
  loading dock and, 134
formaldehyde, 96, 99
  in drop ceilings, 102
  in fabrics, 114
  in flooring, 101, 109
  in insulation, 102–103
  recommendations for, **42**
  wood and, 100, 112, 119, 120
formic acid, in fabrics, 114
framing of building, 23
freezing, in pipes, 53, 54, 102
functional spaces
  auditorium/meeting spaces, 151–152
  computer room, 143
  design criteria for, 153
  elevators, 138–139
  food service/lunchroom, 144–145, 152
  gift shop, 152–153
  laboratories, 139–142
  library, 145
  loading dock, 134–136
  lobby, 149–150
  lockers/locker rooms, 144, 150–151
  offices, 145
  public spaces, 149–153
  rationale for, 133–134
  reading rooms, 145–149
  receiving, 136–137
  restrooms, 144, 151
  service corridors, 138
  shared work spaces, 145
  staff spaces, 144–145
  supply storage, 137–138

visitor service center, 151
funding, public *versus* private, 12, 13
furniture
　materials and finishes for, 110–112, 117
　in reading rooms, 119–120

garage, 29
gas agent fire suppression systems, 53
gaseous contaminants, **42**, 100. *See also* pollutants; volatile organic compounds (VOC)
gaskets, 105, 115
gas-phase filter, 40, 41, 121
general spaces, lighting in, 93–94
gift shop, **81**, 91, 152–153
glass and glazing, 60
　in furniture, **109**, 110
glass plates, photographic, 35
glycol solutions, 37
"green" building, 14, 75
ground level, in construction, 20–21
grout, 117

handicap accessibility, 17
hard drives, 36
heat
　in display cases, 87
　from lighting, 77, 82, 88, 89
heating, ventilation, and air-conditioning (HVAC) systems
　cold and hot water heating, 37
　design of, 27
　electronic controls in, 32, 43
　in long-term cold storage, 32
　pollutants and, 121
　redundancy of, 29
　security of, 59
HEPA. *See* high efficiency particulate filter
*Heritage Health Index on the State of America's Collections* (Institute of Museum and Library Services), 1
high bay storage, 24, 55, 127, 128
high efficiency particulate filter (HEPA), **36**, 40, 41
historic preservation, 13–14
Historic Preservation Act, Section 106 of, 13
holding areas
　design criteria for, 148
　fire suppression in, 55
　lighting in, **80**, 88–89
　materials and finishes in, 107, **107**
　security of, 66
Hollow Metal Manufacturers Association (HMMA), 62
HVAC. *See* heating, ventilation, and air-conditioning (HVAC) systems

Illuminating Engineering Society of North America (IESNA), 90, 93, 94
incandescent lamps, 77, 86, 87
infrared (IR) light, 75, 77, 78, 82
infrared sensors, 71–73
inkjet prints, 35
insects, 25, 29, 136
Institute of Museum and Library Services, 1
insulation, 23, 24, 102–103
integrated pest management, 14
interior, construction of, 23
International Organization for Standardization (ISO), 3, **42**
intruder detection systems, 60, 64, 70–72
isolation
　of fire and smoke, 47
　receiving area and, 137

keys, 63

laboratories
    design criteria for, 139–140
    environmental criteria for, **36**
    equipment in, 141–142
    fire suppression in, 55
    furniture of, 140–141
    lighting in, **80**, 84–86
    location and adjacencies of, 140
    materials and finishes in, 115–118
    size of, 140
    supplies storage in, **36**
    windows in, 60
laboratories, dry, **36**, **80**, 84–85
laboratories, reformatting, **80**, 86
laboratories, special media, **80**, 85
laboratories, wet, **36**, **80**, 85
lacquers, 96
land ownership
    private or public, 12, 13, 14
landscaping, 14–15
latex-based paints, 102, 109, 116, 119
Leadership in Energy and Environmental Design (LEED) Green Building Rating System, 14
library, 145
life safety codes, 19, 20, 45, 126, 127
lighting
    in cold storage, 83
    color and, 75, 76, **80**, 84, 86
    damage caused by, 78–79
    economics of, 76–78
    filters in, 77
    functions of, 79
    heat from, 82, 87, 90
    landscape design and, 14
    levels, **80–81**
    materials and finishes of fixtures, 106–107
    in mixed-use areas, 83–87
    noise from, 89
    rationale for, 75–78
    in reading rooms, 66, 148
    safety of, 78–79
    for security, 72
    security of, 59
    in stacks, 83
light wells, 90, 93
limited-access storage, 33
linen, 114, **114**
loading dock
    design of, 29, 134–135
    doors of, 136
    environmental criteria for, 37
    lighting in, **81**, 92
    location and adjacencies of, 135–136
    security of, 64
loads and loading
    of elevators, 138
    of floors, 24, 124
    of laboratory floors, 139
lobby, 37, **81**, 89–90, 149–150
location
    of loading dock, 135–136
    of mechanical systems, 28, 49–50
lockers/locker room, **81**, 90, 92, 144, 150–151
locks
    electronic or electromagnetic, 61, 63
    on exterior doors, 60
    on lighting/electrical panels, 59
    recommendations for, 67, **68**
    security of, 62–63
low oxygen fire suppression systems, 55–56
lubricants, 106
luminaires, 82, 84, 85

maintenance
    landscape design and, 14
    of mechanical systems, 27, 28
map cases, 106, 130–131

masonry, 47
Material Safety Data Sheets (MSDS), 97, 103
materials and finishes
 in exhibit cases, 112–115
 external building materials, 97–98
 in laboratories, 115–118
 mitigation strategies for, 120–121
 in processing, exhibit, and holding areas, 107–112
 prohibited, 96, 155–156
 rationale for, 95–97
 in reading rooms, 118–120
 selection and testing of, 96–97
 for shelving, 124
 in stacks, 98–106
mat switches, 70
mechanical systems
 design of, 27, 28–29
 environmental, 37–38
 fire and smoke dampers in ducts, 50
 fire protection and, 49–50
 HVAC, 37–38
 location of, 28
meeting rooms. *See* auditorium/training/meeting rooms
MERV filtration, **36–37**. *See also* Minimum Efficiency Reporting Rating
metal furniture, **109**, 110
microfilm, 40
microwave alarms, 71
Minimum Efficiency Reporting Rating (MERV), 40, 41
"Minimum Standard Detail Requirements for ALTA/ACSM Land Title Surveys," 11
mixed-use areas
 air filtration of, 41
 environmental criteria for, 33, 36

lighting in, **80**, 83–87
paper-based records in, 33, 34
moisture control, 21
mold control, 22, 101, 136
monitoring
 of ceilings, 102
 by commissioning agent, 30
 of materials and products, 97
 of windows, 60
*Museum Environment, The* (Thomson), **42**

National Archives and Records Administration (NARA), 39, **42**
 Research and Test Lab of, 97
National Association of Government Archivists and Records Administrators (NAGARA), 5
National Electrical Code (NEC), 50–51
National Environmental Policy Act (NEPA), 10
National Fire Protection Association (NFPA)
 NFPA #10, *Standard for Portable Fire Extinguishers*, 52
 NFPA 13, *Standard for the Installation of Sprinkler Systems*, 53
 NFPA 70, *National Electrical Code*, 50
 NFPA 72, *National Fire Alarm Code*, 50, 51
 NFPA 232, *Standard for the Protection of Records and Storage*, 46
 NFPA 750, *Standard for Water Mist Fire Protection Systems*, 53
 NFPA 909, *Code for the Protection of Cultural Resources*, 46–47, 53
 NFPA 2001, *Standard on*

*Clean Agent Fire Extinguishing Systems,* 53, 55
National Information Standards Organization (NISO), 3, **42**
National Research Council (NRC), **42**
National Society of Professional Surveyors, 11
negative air pressure, 29, 152
neoprene, 105, 115
NFPA. *See* National Fire Protection Association
nitrate-base film, 34
noise, from lighting, 89
non-public spaces, **81**, 92

oak, 100, 120
occupancy sensors, 93
off-gassing, 39, **80**, **81**, 87, 95. *See also* formaldehyde; volatile organic compounds (VOC)
    flooring and, 99, 100, 101
    of metal finishes, 105, 106, 110, 124
    in records areas, 95
    of wood, 100, 110, 120
offices, **81**, 91–92, 145
oil-based paints, 102, 109, 111, 117, 119
openings, exterior, 25
oversized records, 130–131, 147
oxygen, in fires, 55–56
ozone, 39, **42**

paints
    alkyd, 102, 109, 117, 119
    enamel, 104, 106, 107
    latex-based, 102, 109, 116, 119
    oil-based, 102, 109, 111, 117, 119
paper-based records
    environment for, 32–34, **36**, 37, 38, 39

    storage of, 32, 33
parking, 10, 17
perimeter security, 58–59, 69–70, 100
petroleum, 106
photoelectric beams, 66, 71
photographic paper prints, 35
pipes and ducts, 28
    materials and finishes for, 102, 109, 116–117
    stacks and, 50, 59, 102
plastic, 40, 105, 106, 118
plywood, 100, 111, 120
police department, 58, 64, 72 60
pollutants
    filtration of, 39–42
    gaseous, 40–41, **42**
    isolation from sources of, 27, 29
    loading dock and, 134–135
polyester, 106, 113, 114, **114**
polyester-base photographic film, 35
polyester magnetic tape, 36
polyurethane, 100, 110–111, 120
pools and fountains, 15, 25
positive air pressure, 27, 134
powder coated metal, 97, 102, 104, 107, 110
pre-action fire suppression systems, 53, 54
Preservation Environmental Monitors (PEM), 102
processing areas
    design criteria for, 142–143
    environmental criteria for, **36**
    fire suppression in, 55
    gaseous contaminants in, **42**
    lighting in, **80**, 83–84
    materials and finishes in, **107**, 107–112
    windows in, 60
public hearing, 12
public observation windows, 140
public spaces, **42**, **81**, 89–91, 149
pumping systems, 20, 21

racking systems, 131
radon gas, 22
ramp, 134
rate-of-rise thermal detection, 51
reading rooms
    design criteria for, 145–149
    environmental criteria for, 37
    layout of, 65–66
    lighting in, **80**, 87–89, **88**
    materials and finishes in, 118–120
    security of, 64–66
    windows in, 60
reading rooms, audiovisual, 37, **80**, **88**, 149
reading rooms, finding aids room, **80**
reading rooms, microfilm, 37, **80**, **88**, 148–149
reading rooms, records holding, 37, **80**
reading rooms, researcher registration, **80**
reading rooms, textual, 37, **80**, 87–88, 147–148
receiving
    design criteria for, 64, 136–137
    environmental criteria for, 37
    isolation in, 137
    lighting in, **81**, 92
records. *See also* individual types of records
    movement through facility, 133–134
    oversized, 147
reference desk, 147
reformatting rooms
    design criteria for, 142
    environmental criteria for, 36
    lighting levels in, 80
relative humidity, **31**, **121**. *See also* archival environments
    criteria for, **36–37**
    fluctuations in, 38–39
researcher registration/orientation/consultation spaces, 65, **80**, 89, 146–147
researchers
    supervision of, 65–66, 147
    surveillance of, 72–73
Response to Intervention (RTI), 54
restrooms, **81**, 93, 144, 151
risk assessment
    for fire risk, 46
    for security, 12, 14, 58
    in site selection, 8
roof, 16, 25–26
rubber, 115

SAA. *See* Society of American Archivists
sanitary sewer, 16
sealants and coatings
    for concrete, 97, 99
    for exhibit cases, 115
    for wood, 100, 110–111, 120
security
    external, 58–61
    of loading dock, 64
    physical security systems, 67–73
    rationale for, 57–58
    of reading room, 64–66
    risk assessment for, 12, 58
    site, 14
security office, lighting in, **81**, 92
seismic activity, 21, 24, 124
sensors
    infrared, 71–72
    intruder, 60
    occupancy, 77, 90, 93
    stress, 71
    water, 26, 28
service providers, 13
shelving
    bays, 125
    dimensions of, 128–130
    layout of, 126–128

materials and finishes for, 104–106, 124
rails of mobile, 125
in reading rooms, 120
size of shelves, 129–130
spacing of shelves, 129
systems, 123–124
wood, 112
signage, **81**, 94, 106
silica gel, 38, 115
silicone sealants and adhesives, 96, 106, 115, 155
silk, 114, **114**
site design, zoning, 13–14
site selection, 8–9, 10
skylights, 26, 59, 86
smoke detectors, 50, 51
smoke obscuration rates, 51
smoking, **37**, 151
Society of American Archivists (SAA)
Council of, 5
Standards Committee of, 4
soundproofing, 146
spotlights, 79, 93
sprinkler systems, 53, 55, 82
stacks
access to, 31, 66
air filtration for, 40–41
carpets and fabric in, 105
doors of, 49
ducts serving, 50
elevators and stairways in, 49
environmental criteria for, **36**, 37–38
fire extinguishers in, 52
fire hoses and standpipes in, 52
fire safe construction of, 47–49
fire suppression systems in, 53–54
floors in, 98–101, **99**
gaseous contaminants in, **42**
large, 37–38
lighting in, **80**, 82–83

materials and finishes in, 98–106, **104**
mechanical systems for, 49–50
security of, 61–64
small, 38
smoke detection in, 51
walls of, 48
windows in, 59, 63
wood in, 105
staff spaces
design criteria for, 144–145
environmental criteria for, **37**
lighting in, **81**, 91–92
security and, 61
stairways, 49, **81**, 93–94
standards
for carpets, 108, 119
for cultural resources, 46–47
for doors, 49
electrical, 50
environmental, 39, 42
for environmental fluctuations, 39
for fire suppression, 50, 51, 52, 53, 55
for nitrate film storage, 34
for shelving, 124
for site surveys, 11
standpipes and fire hoses, 52
steel
chrome-plated, 104, **104**
countertops, 118
finishes for, 106
in furniture, 117
in lighting fixtures, 107
in shelving and cabinets, 104, **104**
stone, 118
storage
accessories, 130
aisles in, 127–128
anticipating future needs for, 9
boxes, 130
cold, 83

conditions of, 31–32
dimensions of, 128–130
high bay, 24, 128
layout of, 126–128
limited-access, 33
long-term cold, 33, **36**, 55
mixed-use, 33
supply, 137–138
storage equipment
   cabinets, 131
   for cold storage, 131
   construction and performance, 124
   dimensions of, 128–130
   layout of, 126–128
   materials and finishes, 124
   oversized records, 130–131
   rationale, 123
   shelving systems, 123–124
storm drainage system, 16
stress sensors, 71
sulfur and sulfur compounds, 96, 114, 155
sulfur dioxide, **42**
sunlight, 140
supply storage/warehouse, 92
surveillance equipment, 72–73
survey of site, 11
suspended ceilings, 102

tables, 140–141, 143, 147
Task Force on Archival Facilities Guidelines
   of SAA, 4
Teflon, 105, 115
telecommunications systems, 17
temperature. *See also* archival environments
   in computer room, 143
   criteria for, **36–37**
   fluctuations in, 38–39
thermal detection of smoke, 51
Thomson, G., **42**
tile, **99**, 101, **107**, 109, 116, 117
trash, 134, 135, 137, 152
trees, 14, 15
UL. *See* Underwriters Laboratories
ultrasonic devices, 71, 72, 93
ultraviolet (UV) light
   damage from, 75, 77, 78
   in laboratories, 140
   maximum levels of, **80**
   windows and, 60
Underwriters Laboratories (UL)
ANSI/UL 155, *Tests for Fire Resistance of Vault and File Room Doors*, 49
uninterruptible power supply, 143
U.S. Green Building Council, 14
utilities, at building site, 15–17

vapor barriers, 24, 28
vaults, 34
vegetation, 14
ventilation. *See* heating, ventilation, and air-conditioning (HVAC) systems
vermin, 25, 29, 100, 136
vibration detectors, 70
vinyl, 101, 106
visitor service center, 151
volatile organic compounds (VOC), 23, 95, 99, 109. *See also* formaldehyde; off-gassing
   filtration of, 39–40
   in wood, 100, 110–111

walls
   fire protection of, 48
   materials and finishes for, 102, 109, 116–117
   in reading rooms, 119
   of stacks, 48
water intrusion. *See also* flooding
   below ground level, 20–21
   landscaping and, 14
   pools and fountains and, 15
   roofs and, 26

water mist systems, 53
water sensors, 26, 28
water systems and supply, 15, 59
wet-pipe sprinkler systems, 53, 54
windows
    in computer rooms, 143
    in exhibit areas, 86
    in laboratories, 140
    security of, 59–60, 63, 69–70
    UV filters in, 60
wireless networks, 143
WL fixtures, 93
wood
    in exhibit cases, 113
    flooring, **99**, 100, **107**, 108
    in furniture, **109**, 110–111, 117
    in reading rooms, 119
    in shelving and cabinets, **104**, 105
    species of, 120
    in stacks, **104**, 105
wool, 114, **114**
workstations, digital, 149

zones
    in fire suppression systems, 54
    in lighting, 82–83, 90, 93
zoning, 13–14